## ADVANCE PRAISE FOR TRAVELING SOLO

Mary L. Strobbe's *Traveling Solo Later in Life* offers a refreshing perspective on the joys and benefits of solo travel, especially for those whose biological age does not match their spirit. Her writing is accessible and thoughtful, striking a comfortable balance between informative and entertaining. I love her stories, and because the writing style is conversational, it feels a lot like a chat with a knowledgeable friend. Strobbe's work shines in its practical approach to minimizing our footprint, teaching us about ways to make responsible choices while embracing sustainable travel. As someone who lives in a tourist destination, I appreciate that "a country per day" on a cruise ship, blowing through a city in six hours, isn't the best way to go. Strobbe's personal anecdotes add a relatable warmth to the narrative, and, with a focus on both close-to-home and far-flung destinations, this book is an invitation to embrace adventure at any stage of life. Very highly recommended.

~Readers' Favorite 5-star review by Jamie Michele

There is so much good advice for new and seasoned travelers in *Traveling Solo Later in Life*. Strobbe's enthusiasm comes through, and her extensive experiences (positive and negative) have made her quite the expert. She's made mistakes and has learned from them, and by sharing her blunders, others can be prepared and (hopefully) avoid them – especially having a curse put on them!

I especially like her counsel to balance seeing ALL the sights with taking time to relax and enjoy the local culture and daily life at a café or park. Browsing a bookshop can be as interesting as a tourist-filled museum, and you'll get a better feel for the local culture by people watching in non-touristy areas.

While one should take some extra care when traveling alone, one can still wander a bit and explore off the tourist track. Strobbe shows how making a wrong turn can bring travelers to a great neighborhood shop not listed in guidebooks, or how dining alone can inspire new friendships! Strobbe deftly explores the balance of how to stay safe, while having a little courage to try new things and find wonderful adventures!

And I really appreciate the part about self-care and managing anxiety or dealing with depression while traveling. Solo travel is freeing, but it can also get lonely in certain situations (like when I was in Beijing alone during the 2011 earthquake in Japan, and I had no internet in my hotel. All I had for company was Anderson Cooper on the only English TV station with CNN disaster footage). I've never seen any other travel guide with such helpful tips.

~Heather Dorsey, Global Travel Manager for Youth for Understanding International Exchange

*Traveling Solo Later in Life* is the warm, wise, and quietly funny companion every aspiring solo traveler deserves. Aimed at women but helpful for anyone with a suitcase and a sense of curiosity, it offers practical tips on everything from trip planning and safety to emotional wellness and sneaky hotel-room exercises. The personal stories are equal parts heartwarming and hilarious—proof that travel, like life, rarely goes according to plan (and that's half the fun). Whether you're dreaming of far-off adventures or dipping a toe in with a staycation, this book is your gentle nudge to go for it, and for yourself.

~Paul Hill, Global wanderer

*Traveling Solo Later in Life* by Mary Strobbe, PhD, is an insightful guide that blends personal anecdotes, practical advice, and emotional encouragement into a compelling ode to independent travel. With a tone that is both conversational and wise, the book captures the author's enthusiasm for solo journeys while equipping readers with tools to travel safely, smartly, and joyfully. Strobbe vividly illustrates the appeal of solo travel: the freedom to follow your whims, discover your capabilities, and savor unexpected conversations and personal insights.

*Traveling Solo Later in Life* offers practical, well-organized, and actionable sections on planning, packing light, navigating international finances, choosing lodging, and handling safety. These tips are never dry; they're woven into entertaining stories. Even Strobbe's run-ins with language barriers and airport snafus are presented with humor and humility. Beyond logistics, the book addresses deeper resilience, self-discovery, and empowerment themes. The reflections on aging and accessibility are thoughtful, with anecdotes that honor both limitations and possibilities. Mary Strobbe champions adaptability and preparation, reminding readers that solo travel has no age or ability limits with the right mindset and planning. While personal, the book avoids being insular. The author draws on experiences from around the globe. Cultural insights are shared with respect and curiosity, reinforcing that travel is more than destinations; it's about relationships, even fleeting ones, with people and places. This is an empowering, practical, and heartfelt resource for anyone considering venturing alone. Readers who enjoy memoirs, travel essays, or guides with a deeply personal touch will find this book both useful and inspiring. I highly recommend this engaging book.

~ Readers' Favorite 5-star review by Carol Thompson

*Traveling Solo Later in Life* is part guidebook, part memoir—and fully empowering. While it speaks directly to female solo travelers, this engaging and informative book offers a wealth of practical advice for anyone with a passport and a sense of curiosity, regardless of age or gender. A seasoned traveler will appreciate its planning checklists, emotional wellness tips, and even clever in-room exercises (yes, your hotel lamp might double as a stretch partner).

~Alister Ramírez Márquez, Author My Emerald Green Dress

*Traveling Solo Later in Life* is a warm and practical blend of personal stories, travel advice, and reflections on independence through solo travel. Mary L. Strobbe takes readers through her journeys across continents, sharing everything from packing tips and booking strategies to cultural insights and safety practices. Each chapter tackles a specific theme — like transportation, lodging, communication, finance, and even health — with anecdotes from her experiences. The book is particularly geared toward older adults and solo female travelers, with honest stories that show the joys and challenges of navigating the world alone. The inclusion of photographs—not just scenic travel shots but also pictures of the author, currency, and local scenes—gives it the feel of a well-loved travel journal rather than a dry how-to guide. This book is both insightful and enjoyable, offering a thoughtful mix of humor, honesty, and practical advice.

One of the book's biggest strengths is its structure: short chapters, clear subheadings, and bullet points make it easy to read and revisit. Each section is themed, so readers can go straight to topics like safety, communication, or packing tips, depending on what they need. Mary L. Strobbe's voice is calm, funny, and experienced. She isn't afraid to share moments of vulnerability, such as losing her phone in Copenhagen or nearly getting cursed at in Cuba. These authentic experiences make her advice more trustworthy and grounded. The tone strikes an outstanding balance between informative and personal. It doesn't talk down to the reader, nor does it try too hard to be clever. Strobbe speaks directly to older women, a demographic often overlooked in travel writing. She addresses common fears and limitations without being patronizing. There's genuine encouragement in these pages, the kind that says: "You can absolutely do this — and here's how." That empowering message, backed by lived experience, makes the book truly inspiring. *Traveling Solo Later in Life* is Ideal for women 50+, new solo travelers, or anyone craving independence through travel.

~Readers' Favorite 5-star review by Manik Chaturmutha

# TRAVELING SOLO LATER IN LIFE

MARY STROBBE

Copyright © 2025 by Mary Strobbe

All rights reserved.

Published by Konstellation Press, San Diego

www.konstellationpress.com

No part of this book may be reproduced in any form or by any electronic or mechanical means, including information storage and retrieval systems, without written permission from the author, except for the use of brief quotations in a book review.

ISBN: 979-8-9908181-4-9

*"To my fabulous feline companions, who prefer the comforts of home over wild escapades, and who patiently (and sometimes passive-aggressively) await my return—with purrs pending."*

# CONTENTS

*Introduction* — xiii
*Introduction* — xv
*Travel Insurance, Medical Insurance, Evacuation* — xxi

Chapter 1 — 1
Communications — 7
Chapter 2 — 8
Money — 15
Chapter 3 — 16
Safety — 25
Chapter 4 — 26
Travel Documents — 33
Chapter 5 — 34
Accessibility when Traveling — 39
Chapter 6 — 40
Air Transportation — 47
Chapter 7 — 48
Lodging — 55
Chapter 8 — 56
Food — 67
Chapter 9 — 68
Cruises — 79
Chapter 10 — 80
Trains, Taxis and Other Forms of Transportation — 89
Chapter 11 — 90
Tours — 97
Chapter 12 — 98
SPAS — 103
Chapter 13 — 104
Ecotourism — 111
Chapter 14 — 112
Physical and Mental Health — 117

| | |
|---|---|
| Chapter 15 | 118 |
| Staycation | 123 |
| Chapter 16 | 124 |
| Epilogue | 129 |
| *The Great Solo Expedition* | 131 |
| *Appendices* | 137 |
| *Packing* | 143 |
| *Signals That You Might Be a U.S. Tourist* | 145 |
| *Resources* | 149 |
| *Places to Start Your Solo Adventures* | 151 |
| *Exercise Disclaimer* | 155 |
| *Managing Anxiety While Traveling* | 161 |
| *Afterword* | 167 |
| *Sample Itinerary* | 173 |
| *Acknowledgments* | 177 |
| *About the Author* | 179 |

# INTRODUCTION

Leopold Kron Schloss, Salzburg, Austria

*Trying to determine what is going on in the world by reading newspapers is like trying to tell the time by watching the second hand of a clock." Ben Hecht*

# INTRODUCTION

## THE LIBERATING ADVENTURE OF BEING YOUR OWN BEST TRAVEL BUDDY

Solo travel is an intoxicating blend of emotions—excitement, freedom, challenge and reward. Each journey becomes a story uniquely shaped by you. When you're in charge, every decision, from where to go to how long to linger in a cozy café or to follow a winding trail on a whim adds a personal touch to your adventure. Solo travel places you firmly in the driver's seat where the possibilities are as vast as your imagination.

Solo travel is an adventure like no other, an exhilarating cocktail of self-discovery, and the occasional moment of wondering, *What on earth have I gotten myself into?* It's not just about visiting new places; it's about meeting a version of yourself that you didn't even know existed. When you're traveling alone, there's no buffer, no backup, and no one else to blame if things go awry—which is exactly what makes it so thrilling.

For me, planning an adventure is a delightful ritual: a combination of meticulous logistics and dreamy wanderlust. It often begins with the essentials, like arranging lodging and money, but quickly turns into a map of personal aspirations. After years of letting work schedules dictate my trips, I now relish the freedom to choose based on seasons, special events, or even a book club meeting I can't bear to miss.

I design a trip entirely around my whims, whether that means spending hours wandering through a local market, hopping on a bus to nowhere in particular or sitting by the beach with a book I've been meaning to read for months. It's an antidote to the monotony of routine, a reminder that life is full of possibilities and the world is far more welcoming than it sometimes seems.

**The Art of Planning: Spreadsheets Meet Daydreams**

I have a confession: I love planning trips almost as much as I love taking them. For me, the process starts with a blank slate and an open mind. Sometimes it's a practical decision — timing a trip to catch the cherry blossoms in Washington, D.C. or escaping winter with a jaunt to Mexico City. Other times, it's pure serendipity: a photo on social media, a recommendation from a stranger or even a novel set in a faraway land that sparks my curiosity.

The planning itself is part precision, part poetry. I have spreadsheets that would impress an accountant, filled with everything from flight options to obscure local festivals. But I also leave space for the kind of spontaneity that solo travel thrives on. What's the point of crossing off a checklist if you can't veer off course when a charming alleyway or irresistible café catches your eye?

Of course, there's also the joy of being a little selfish. After years of coordinating vacations around other people's preferences, solo travel feels like a delicious indulgence. No compromises, no debates, no "Do we really need to go to the museum of chocolate?" If I want to spend the day in a bookstore or linger in a park with nothing but my thoughts, there's no one to stop me.

**The Delight of Being the Boss**

Solo travel is freedom in its purest form. You're in charge of every detail, from where to go to how long to stay. That said, there's also no one to remind you when you've overindulged at lunch and still have a five-mile hike ahead. It's a double-edged sword, but one I'm more than willing to wield.

I'll never forget a group tour I joined in my early days of travel. It was Thailand and we were promised an "authentic local experience." Instead, we were shepherded into tourist traps selling overpriced trinkets and the temple I'd been dreaming of visiting was nothing more than a distant blur through the bus window.

Worst of all, a charming local struck up a conversation about the city's architecture but before we could exchange more than a few words, the guide hustled us away. If I'd been traveling alone, I could have stayed, chatted, and possibly discovered an insider's view of the city.

Now, those moments of spontaneity and personal connection define my journeys. Solo travel allows me to savor the freedom to pause, pivot, or immerse myself wherever the road — or conversation — leads.

**Challenges and The Art of Packing Light**

Solo travel isn't just about choosing your destination — it's about navigating every part of the journey, from figuring out transportation to solving the occasional hiccup. Group tours may offer the convenience of someone else stepping in

INTRODUCTION

when things go wrong, but there's a distinct satisfaction in handling challenges on your own.

I'll never forget the time I found myself in Venice at midnight, staring at the Grand Canal with my suitcase and no obvious way across. A young man offered to help. Did I hesitate? Of course! For a moment, but after a quick mental inventory (my luggage wasn't exactly filled with crown jewels) I let him assist. He didn't run off with my bag. I left with a valuable lesson: sometimes trusting your instincts pays.

Then there's the art of packing — a critical skill for solo travelers. Without a group to carry the weight (literally), you quickly learn to pack light or face the glares of fellow passengers as you wrestle a suitcase into an overhead bin. On occasion, a chivalrous stranger might step in, though I suspect it's less about saving me and more about avoiding a mid-air suitcase catastrophe.

**Easing Into the Solo Travel Life**

The thought of traveling alone feels overwhelming at first. But here's a little trick: reframe your nervousness as excitement. Instead of thinking, "I'm scared," tell yourself, "I'm thrilled!" That mental shift can make all the difference.

Solo travel doesn't have to be a leap into the deep end. Start small. Book a staycation in your city, ideally at a hotel in the tourist district. Spend a weekend exploring attractions you might otherwise overlook, dine solo, and plan your day entirely on your terms.

Think of it like stepping into a cold pool. Some people ease in gradually, getting used to the water one step at a time, while others dive in with a splash. Both methods work; it's about finding the approach that feels right for you. Each small step builds your confidence and before you know it, that staycation could evolve into a week-long cross-country adventure or even a solo trip abroad.

Solo travel, much like anything new, thrives on familiarity. The more you do it, the more comfortable you become. Just as a once-intimidating grocery store feels routine after a few visits, traveling alone becomes second nature with practice. Each trip reinforces your ability to navigate unfamiliar places, connect with new people and savor the joy of your own company.

**Traveling solo doesn't mean being lonely**

Traveling solo creates opportunities for personal connection that may not be possible with a group. There is something about being alone that makes you more approachable — whether it's a friendly local eager to share hidden gems or a fellow traveler keen on swapping stories. Hotel breakfast buffets, lines at events and communal tables become perfect settings for spontaneous conversations.

The true magic of solo travel lies in the freedom it provides:

- **Exploring at your own pace**: Spend hours in a museum or leave after ten minutes — it's your call.
- **Following your instincts**: Detour down that intriguing alleyway just because it feels right.
- **Setting your schedule**: Early bird or night owl, you're on your own time.
- **Adjusting as you go**: Take a nap, power through, or completely change plans based on your mood.
- **Discovering hidden gems**: Some of the best experiences aren't in any guidebook.

- **Returning with stories**: The good, the bad, and the outright hilarious all become part of your travel tapestry.

Solo travel builds confidence, nurtures independence and carves out rare moments of reflection amidst life's chaos. It's not just about seeing the world — it's about discovering yourself. With every challenge overcome and every new experience, your sense of capability grows, and the world feels a little more accessible.

**Looking Ahead**

For now, the key is to take that first step. Whether it's a weekend getaway or a month-long adventure, solo travel is your chance to embrace the world on your terms. And if anyone asks why you're going alone, just smile, and say, "*Because I can.*"

# TRAVEL INSURANCE, MEDICAL INSURANCE, EVACUATION

*On Moon Pyramid, Teotihuacan, Mexico*

*"Travel is the only thing you buy that makes you richer."*
*Anonymous*

# CHAPTER 1

## *A* Climb, A Fall, and the Teotihuacan Trifecta

When a friend and I booked a day trip to Teotihuacan, we were both excited to see the ancient pyramids just outside Mexico City. She was determined to climb to the very top of the Sun Pyramid — a challenge that didn't tempt me in the slightest. I had tackled the Moon Pyramid on a previous trip and, to be honest, I felt no need to tempt fate a second time. So, I played the supportive spectator role, snapping photos and cheering her on from the sidelines.

Little did I know, my decision to skip the climb wasn't just laziness — it was pure survival instinct.

On her triumphant descent, just a few steps away from solid ground, my friend lost her footing and fell. Hard. In the blink of an eye, she was unable to put any weight on her right foot. Suddenly, our archaeological adventure turned into an unplanned medical drama.

Enter the security guards — two broad-shouldered gentlemen who, for all I know, may moonlight as pyramid guardians. They carried her to the nearest transport with the grace and determination of ancient gods assisting a fallen mortal. From there, it was a short ride to a hospital emergency room where X-rays confirmed the damage. The prescription? Pain medication, a wrapped foot, and a very chic medical boot.

### A Hotel with Heroes

Our return to the hotel wasn't as triumphant as we'd imagined it would be. For one, our room was located up a flight of stairs and my now-booted friend wasn't about to hop her way up there. On top of that, the thought of navigating Mexico City at night to find crutches and Gatorade had my stress levels skyrocketing.

The hotel staff stepped in like knights in shining armor. They found crutches, tracked down Gatorade and even carried my friend upstairs to our room. It was the kind of hospitality you read about in glowing online reviews but rarely experience firsthand.

The next morning, the hotel staff went above and beyond yet again. They arranged for a ride to the airport and made sure a wheelchair was waiting for her at the terminal. It was the kind of send-off usually reserved for royalty — or, in this case, an injured traveler with a great story to tell.

### A First-Class Medical Review

Once she was safely back home, her doctor reviewed the X-rays and treatment provided by the Mexican medical team. His verdict? He wouldn't have changed a thing. And here's the cherry on top: The tour company ended up covering all her medical expenses. It was a happy ending to a not-so-happy fall.

### The Travel Insurance Trifecta

My friend managed to hit the trifecta of travel mishaps: medical emergency, trip interruption and evacuation. Thankfully, her fall didn't involve any bungee jumping, ziplining, or tequila-fueled dancing — activities that would have voided most travel insurance policies. (For the daredevils out there, extreme sports insurance is a must)

Trip interruption insurance could have covered some non-refundable costs, like her ticket to the Ballet Folklórico, but filing a claim for small amounts can sometimes feel more exhausting than the trip itself. Cancel-for-any-reason insurance is another option, though it's pricier and needs to be purchased as soon as you start booking.

### The Case for Medical Evacuation

Medical evacuation coverage is where travel insurance earns its keep. Without it, a medical emergency requiring an airlift home can cost $250,000 or more — a number that still makes me shudder. Years ago, after one too many close calls involving wet tiles and rogue glass, I decided to invest in a lifetime evacuation policy. It's not cheap, but the peace of mind it brings is worth every penny.

### Wet Tiles and Travel Tales

Let me share my own cautionary tale from Ixtapan de la Sal, Mexico. One misstep on a slick surface and I was down in a heap, glass shattering around me like a dramatic movie scene. The result? A gash so deep I got an anatomy lesson on the tendon in my left hand.

This was clearly not a "put a band aid on it" situation. Off I went to the local doctor who cleaned the wound with a precision that suggested either years of practice or a side hustle in fine art restoration. He numbed the area, stitched me up, and then — wait for it — decided he wasn't satisfied with his work. He removed the stitches and started over, adding a few extras for good measure.

The cost for this perfectionism? A mere $100. No paperwork, no insurance hassles — just a flawless recovery. Today, I couldn't point out the scar if I tried. That doctor not only saved my hand but also gave me a story that's equal parts gratitude and humor.

### Travel Insurance: **The Fine Print**

Some credit cards offer limited travel insurance, but the coverage often applies only to purchases made with that card. And the fine print? It's practically a novel requiring a magnifying glass to read. For lost or stolen items, your homeowner's insurance might provide some coverage so it's worth checking before you invest in additional policies.

The cost of travel insurance depends on factors like your age, cost of the trip and trip's duration, your destination and the activities you plan to do. (Hint: Cuba won't even let you in without proof of medical insurance and cruise lines often require it as part of the booking process.)

Choosing the right insurance can feel like solving a Rubik's Cube in the dark, but it's essential. Whether you're scaling pyramids, ziplining through jungles, or just walking across a wet tile floor, having the right coverage can turn a potential disaster into a great story.

Because if there's one thing travel has taught me, it's this: Surprises are inevitable. Preparation, on the other hand, is optional — but it really shouldn't be.

# COMMUNICATIONS

*La Santora, Havanna, Cuba*

"The woman who follows the crowd will usually go no further than the crowd. The woman who walks alone is like herself in places no one has ever been before." Albert Einstein

# CHAPTER 2

### Adventures in Multilingual Chaos

When I arrived at my hotel in Athens, the friendly receptionist handed me a room key — a hefty six-inch slab of metal that could double as a doorstop or perhaps a blunt weapon in an emergency. It was inscribed with what I could only describe as Greek hieroglyphics. Adding to the charm, the room numbers were written in the Greek alphabet. Armed with my key and a healthy dose of misplaced confidence, I wandered the hallways, squinting at signs and doors, hoping for divine intervention or, at the very least, a room that looked vaguely inviting.

After a solid five minutes of aimless meandering during which I passed the same confused-looking tourist twice, I admitted defeat. With a resigned sigh, I trudged back to the reception desk, holding up the key like an archaeologist presenting a mysterious artifact. "Help," I mumbled, my tone somewhere between sheepish and desperate.

This, as it turned out, this was just the prologue to my linguistic escapades across Greece, Turkey, Italy, and France.

While I felt moderately prepared for Paris — thanks to my prior trips to France, which, though rusty, could scrape me through basic interactions — Greek and Turkish were different. A few Italian words would carry me through.

Attempting to learn even a handful of words felt like trying to decode an alien language. But I persisted, focusing on what I deemed the essentials: two words per language: "hello" and "no." It's a minimalist approach to linguistics and while it won't win you any awards for cultural fluency, it's surprisingly effective for day-to-day survival.

### The Power of Six Words

If you are bi- or multi-lingual, congratulations. If not, do not let it prevent you from exploring the world. Six words will go far: hello, good-bye, please, thank you, yes and most importantly, NO.

For those of us who aren't bilingual or multilingual, don't despair. You don't need to master entire conjugations to explore the world. Need to add a bit of situational flair? Toss in "help," "doctor," "restroom," and "police," just in case your adventures take an unexpected turn (which, let's be honest, they can).

Any effort made speaking their language is appreciated even if mispronounced. It is the effort that is valued, showing respect for their culture. Take comfort knowing the linguistics are best acquired in pre-pubescence. It's a little late now to master another language. But that should not stop any effort to learn a few basic words. On occasion, you might even spark a connection as they correct you with a smile or, in some cases, a hearty laugh that somehow feels more endearing than condescending.

## Speaking Like a Local (Almost)

One of my proudest linguistic triumphs unfolded in Paris. Staying in a charming, slightly creaky apartment, I established a morning ritual: shuffling to the *boulangerie* around the corner in my pajamas, concealed under a shearling coat and accessorized with Ugg boots. Armed with a well-rehearsed "bonjour" and a carefully enunciated "merci," I'd confidently order croissants or a palmier, pretending I was a local — albeit one with a suspiciously touristy aura.

The bakery staff, bless them, never let on that they knew the truth. Instead, they smiled, nodded and handed me my pastries as if I'd mastered the art of blending in. For those brief moments, I felt a sense of belonging, a fleeting illusion of being one with the Parisians.

## Nonverbal Communication: A Field Guide to Awkwardness

Words are important, sure, and gestures can often speak louder, but unfortunately, they can also backfire spectacularly. Gestures that are friendly or neutral in one culture can be downright offensive in another. For example, in Greece, a nod might mean "no," while shaking your head could mean "yes." It's a delightful reversal that kept me perpetually confused. Meanwhile, in Turkey, showing the sole of your shoe is considered impolite, and in Thailand, patting a child on the head is seen as bringing bad luck to the child. During a trip to Cuba, a miscommunication spiraled into something...unexpected. My camera bag, in all its clumsy glory, managed to disrupt a *Santería* altar. The altar's keeper, *La*

TRAVELING SOLO LATER IN LIFE

*Santora*, was less than pleased and her grandson solemnly informed me that she had put a curse on me. A curse?! On me? Horrified and utterly speechless, I stood there, trying to process the situation.

Does this black magic even exist? What does science say? I tried to think logically because, you know, logic always helps when you're potentially cursed in a foreign country. (Spoiler: it doesn't.)

As our group of photographers prepared to leave, the grandson approached me again with a surprising update. "Grandma says you have a good heart," he said, "but you should throw some fruit into the ocean to appease the *Orishas*." These spirits influence both nature and humans. Thus, an action was warranted to ward off any bad vibes.

So, what did I do? I threw an apple and an orange into the ocean. Not in Cuba, mind you, but later in Encinitas. Because, honestly, how does one measure the impact of negative forces on one's life? I was not about to take any chance.

Even in English-speaking countries, accents and local slang can turn communication into a delightful puzzle. I vividly recall a New Year's Eve in Glasgow, where I learned about Hogmanay traditions, sampled haggis and attempted to decode a kilt-wearing Scot's thick brogue. While I didn't catch every word, his enthusiasm and warmth were unmistakable, proving that even when language fails, human connection prevails.

**CELL PHONES: Your Best Friend and Worst Enemy**

Traveling with a cell phone is both a blessing and a curse. On the one hand, it's an indispensable tool for navigation, communication and, occasionally, Googling "How do I say, 'Where is the bathroom?'" On the other hand, a cellphone can lead to financial ruin if you're not careful.

I have "lost" my phone numerous times. Once in Copenhagen and another time at a Paris Christmas market. In Copenhagen I was not aware it was missing and an honest marketer at the airport asked me if it was mine as he showed it to me. In Paris I had to retrace my steps and was able to find it at the warm glogg stall.

Many years ago, I learned this the hard way, naively assuming that Wi-Fi was free and unlimited, I streamed content on a train ride from London to Edinburgh. The resulting phone bill was a traumatic life event — equivalent to a mortgage payment or two. After several tearful calls to my carrier, I managed to negotiate a reduction, but the experience left me scarred; and considerably poorer.

Thankfully, options have improved since then. International plans, local eSIM cards, and free messaging apps like WhatsApp can save you from financial disaster. And if you're particularly tech-savvy, consider using a VPN to protect your data on public networks. Translation apps are also a godsend, though it's best to keep your phrases simple. Think toddler grammar: subject, verb, done.

### Embracing the Missteps

Ultimately, travel isn't about perfection; it's about connection. Whether you're fumbling with Greek hotel keys, mangling basic phrases, or engaging in a spirited game of charades with a local shopkeeper, these moments are what make the journey memorable

So, pack your six essential words, a healthy dose of

humility, and an oversized sense of humor. You won't always get it right, but that's the beauty of it. Missteps and misunderstandings often lead to the best stories — the kind you'll laugh about for years to come.

And while technology will continue to evolve, no app or gadget can replace the joy of a shared moment with someone across cultures. Whether your "thank you" earns a bemused chuckle or your "hello" is met with unexpected enthusiasm, these small connections are what truly make the adventure worthwhile.

### Final Thoughts

As individuals, we each have varying levels of comfort and ability when it comes to technology, which often seems to evolve faster than we do. It's perfectly okay not to keep up with every rapid change; many of us simply aren't interested. Stick to the tools and devices you're comfortable using. Travel, especially solo travel, is not the ideal time to experiment with or master unfamiliar technology. Instead, focus on what works for you and what helps you feel confident and prepared.

# MONEY

*Cuban Pesos*

*"Jobs fill your pocket; **ADVENTURES** fill your soul." Jaime Lyn Beatty*

# CHAPTER 3

*P*assport? Check. Clean Bills? Check.

In Buenos Aires, a friend made repeated trips between the money changer booth and her hotel several blocks away because she failed to bring her passport (she had waited in line over 20 minutes to discover a passport was required), then again because her money was "dirty," "torn" or had writing on it. Returning with the passport it was another 20-plus minutes to learn that her Euros were unacceptable. (So, laundering your money could be a good thing?)

### CREDIT AND DEBIT Card Wisdom

Notify your bank of your travels if you expect to be able to use your credit cards abroad. This can be done online with some banks. One exception I know is the USAA bank which does not require notification; most of their members are military and their descendants. Frequent and sudden relocations are a fact of life for the military.

To use your credit card, it must have a chip and the standard four-digit pin. The pin issued with one of my cards was six digits. Four numbers are the maximum, so I asked the bank to change it. Do not carry all your credit cards with you when traveling. I suggest at least two different credit cards; one Master Card and one Visa. (Not all merchants accept American Express.) Use credit cards that have no foreign transaction fees. I am reluctant to carry a debit card. If it is stolen or scanned the thieves have access to your bank account.

### CASH? Best Conversion Rate?

There is no advantage to carrying wads of cash with you when you travel. ATMs are available in most countries. Looking for an ATM (sometimes called "Bank Machines") can be like a treasure hunt. In my travels I have found them "hidden" inside stores, as happened in Oslo and parts of Mexico.

Unable to find an ATM, my next reasonable choice is a bank. Exchanging money at a bank in foreign countries is complicated and takes time, but more secure than getting involved with the Black Market. In Johannesburg, I spent a couple of hours exchanging money due to the extensive forms required, needed to be completed and then documented with official stamps. Exchange houses and kiosks have a very poor rate of exchange and should only be a last resort.

In my experience, ATMs typically offer the best exchange rate—one that closely aligns with the market rate, which isn't directly available to consumers. I use the XE Currency app (money exchange, transfer and converter) on my iPhone to check the current rate for comparison.

Another often-overlooked option is the hotel. While not all hotels offer currency exchange, I've found that some do—and their rates can be surprisingly competitive.

Covid has changed the world in many ways and the "touchless" mode of paying is now the norm. When traveling post Covid, I only need the currency of the country for tips. Even an ice cream cone can be purchased with a credit card in Krakow.

### Hide and Seek: **Stashing your Cash**

Once safe in your hotel room, distribute your money into different locations. Stash some in pockets, wallet, shoe or your money belt. I am not a fan of money belts because when you run out of cash during a purchase, and must open it, how can you do so privately? A restroom is not always nearby or available.

If you are traveling to only one country it is worth learning the currency prior to departure. Guidebooks often have pictures of the different denominations to assist you in familiarizing yourself with the currency. The internet is an excellent resource. Just type in the country and the word "currency".

### Choose Local Currency **Every time**

When a merchant asks if you wish to be charged in USD (U.S. Dollars) or the local currency, choose the local currency. The exchange to dollars can be a disadvantage to you. For example, the person writing the bill calculates the exchange according to their knowledge, which may not be accurate. Your bank will take that charge in dollars as the correct amount. However, if you ask to be charged in local currency, the bank will convert the exchange according to the official exchange rate at the time they receive the charge.

Leaving a country, you can exchange your money back to dollars but be aware the exchange rate is not to your advantage. In Russia I purchased enough candy at the airport to rid myself of my remaining Rubles. I tend to keep my Euros, Pounds Sterling and Mexican Pesos as the likelihood of returning to the countries using that currency is great. However, Cuba requires all Cuban money be exchanged back to your currency. They want to keep all their coins and paper currency in the country. Cuba has two monetary systems, one for residents and one for tourists. Depending on the country of origin the exchange rate can fluctuate. Canadians get a better rate than US citizens.

### ROBBED IN PARADISE

My first night in Jamaica I was robbed of all my cash while I was sitting by the pool enjoying the balmy weather. Nothing else was taken. It could have ruined my trip. Waiting for the police in Jamaica could take hours, if they even made an appearance. Instead, I decided to move on, ask for a room that was not on the ground floor and reframe the incident: Someone needed that money more than I. (This is one very good reason not to accept a ground floor room.)

In Cape Town, my credit cards were missing from my room. I spent hours with hotel security and South African police. I suggest you take a photo of the front and back of your cards. That makes it easy to call the companies to report them stolen. There were no unauthorized charges, but wasted hours with hotel management and police when I could have been discovering the world outside the hotel.

## SAFES: **Friend or Foe?**

The usual recommendation to secure your valuables is to use the room safe or the hotel safe. After I failed trying to retrieve items from my room safe in Ürgüp, Turkey and again in Cabo San Lucas, Mexico, I no longer use room safes. It took the hotel security all of two seconds to open the room safe with a tool he carried. The hotel safe is more secure. Make sure you get a receipt detailing the items you have stored there.

I prefer to place my valuables in my locked luggage. Luggage locks can be cut too, but a special tool is required and if the locks are of quality, it is a long, slow process. In Lisbon, I had to have the lock on my luggage cut because no matter how many combinations I tried, I was unable to open it. That taught me to test out new locks before using them.

## STICKY FINGERS **and Scams**

Theft can and does happen anywhere in the world. Just be vigilant. Keep purses closed or zipped and close in your front. Be aware of pick pockets and scams. If you see a sign cautioning about pick pockets, do not draw attention to your money by placing a hand on it to check on its presence. What you have just done is told the pickpocket where to target. Consider clothing with multiple hidden pockets so you can forgo the purse or use a cross-body purse.

. . .

## BUDGET LIKE A PRO (Not an Optimist)

In budgeting for travels, understand there will be additional expenses you have not considered. There are costs in preparing for your trip at home as well. Do not be lulled into believing the total cost of your trip is simply going to be the cost of any tours, lodging, food and transportation. Those are the big ones, but the small ones add up. Costs to consider are:

- Transportation to and from the airport, departure point or parking fees if you drove yourself.
- Cost for pet care
- Money exchange fees; credit card fees
- Tips
- Use of restroom and toilet paper
- Transportation at location
- Meals, snacks, drinks, water
- Entrance fees
- Souvenirs
- Travel insurance
- WIFI
- Pre-trip purchases of specialized clothing
- Pre-trip purchases of sunscreen and other personal items

Tipping practices vary by country. It is common practice in European countries but almost nonexistent in Asian countries. Japan and China consider it offensive to tip.

In Europe a service charge is often added to the bill. European wait staff are paid well, and you will note they are not young college students as we find in the U.S. They are career professionals who often retire from the position.

. . .

### The Art of Haggling (and Not Offending)

Bargaining or haggling is a way of life in many developing countries. By bargaining we are NOT taking food away from people's mouths but helping maintain some stability in their economy.

A situation that has always made me uncomfortable is photographing people on the street and paying them to allow me to do so. This was poignant in the Sacred Valley of Peru at an outdoor market: a weathered older woman sat at a stall with an array of colorful powders that screamed "photo op!" As I approached her with my DSL camera, she held out her hand indicating she wished to be paid. I offered her an amount in Sols, which I felt was fair. She vigorously shook her finger, indicating "no". I offered another coin, still, the finger shakes "no". Frustrated with me, she lifted the cloth on her table and revealed a stash of coins larger than any I had offered. I walked away. Much later, when I was walking around and at a distance, I used the telephoto lens to capture a photo. Just not the perspective I had imagined.

### Shopping Smart (and Light)

When traveling, most of us love to shop and want to take home mementos and gifts for family and friends. While that four-foot Buddha carving may be perfect on your patio, getting it home is a serious problem. Not all shops will mail. Mail in some areas is not reliable.

My strategy is to find items small and easy to pack made by locals. Some items I tend to purchase are jewelry, scarves, foodstuffs, artwork, and clothing. I was not always that wise and have several wooden and stone carvings that were tricky to get home.

Do your homework in advance to learn what products are specific to the region in which you will be traveling. For example, it would be criminal not to purchase silver jewelry in Taxco, Mexico, the home of the silver mines and numerous silver factories.

### Customs and **VAT**

Reentering the U.S. when you go through customs it is mandatory to declare your purchases. Listing small items as miscellaneous gifts or souvenirs is acceptable Those over the limit ($800 at this time) will incur a tax of 3%.

Keep receipts and the purchase available for customs. If you have paid a VAT (Value Added Tax) there is a refund. This can be done at the airport or via mail once home. In Cabo, they have a station inside an upscale mall that can record the requisite information. When paid by credit card there will be a credit on your statement.

# SAFETY

Grand Bazaar, Istanbul

"A woman is like a tea bag — you can't tell how strong she is until you put her in hot water." attributed to Eleanor Roosevelt but not verified

# CHAPTER 4

## Trust your Gut...and Maybe Leave the Raw Food Alone

As women we are familiar with the basics of traveling solo: Be vigilant, walk with a purpose, keep your purse closed and near your body in front of you, don't reveal detailed information about yourself, trust your" gut," and keep your wits about you...as in do not become inebriated. Pay attention to this advice, but there is more.

I knew the phrase: peel it, cook it or forget it. Did I follow those instructions? No, the fresh fruit at the hotel breakfast buffet looked and smelled so delicious. I indulged. Hours later I was forced to stay in my hotel room, then hours searching for a Pharmacia for Imodium.

## Water, Water Everywhere...But Not a Drop on Your Toothbrush

Keeping hydrated is vital. When the quality of the water is questionable, do not drink it. Hotels concerned about the safety of water will provide complimentary bottles in your room. Should you require more, just ask housekeeping. Four-star hotels may provide bottled water, but they charge for it, which indicates to me their tap water is safe.

In the shower, do not drink any water. At no time allow even a drop of tap water on your toothbrush or in your mouth. A friend and I were careless at the end of a trip and rinsed our toothbrushes with water from the faucet. Home, we each ended up in the emergency room for dehydration, diarrhea and nausea. Frequent Mexico travelers though we were, Montezuma's Revenge caught up with us after all these years.

### Shortcut to Nowhere: The Milan Incident

Walking alone at night in most places is unwise. My near miss was when I thought I knew a shortcut from La Scala (in Milan) to my hotel, but discovered I was mistaken. Lost on a dimly lit and empty street, I heard footsteps behind me. When I sped up or slowed, the footsteps mimicked me. I stopped and so did the footsteps. Turning around and assuming a defensive position, I glared at him. He disappeared across the street and into a side alley. He had no knowledge of my confidence and ability to defend myself. Still, my action alerted him that I was not easy prey. Several years ago, I took a self-defense class called IMPACT that instilled defensive muscle memory. That is what took over when I turned around to face my potential attacker. Screaming is less effective than yelling. Think about it. How do you react to a scream when you hear it? And your reaction to a yell?

. . .

### Dinner Dates and Detective Work

When accepting an invitation for dinner or drinks from locals or fellow travelers take precautions. Write the name of the person(s), the phone number and any other contact information you have down on paper. Include the destination. Prominently display this information in your hotel room, perhaps in the middle of the bed. If the person insists meeting at the hotel, do so only in the lobby where hotel staff can see them. Should you turn up missing, the police will have somewhere to start.

### Night Owls Need Plans Too

Just because you are a solo traveler there is no need to confine yourself to the hotel once it becomes dark. There is much to experience. Aside from a nice dinner I have attended opera, theatre, ballet, symphony, jazz and other musical performances. Be sure to make plans for your return to the hotel. Check how late public transportation runs. Ask the hotel concierge what issues you might encounter attending the event. It was necessary to cancel a dinner reservation in the Asian section of Istanbul because the boat back to the European side where my hotel was did not run late enough to accommodate my schedule.

I did not plan well while attending outdoor performances in Athens and Istanbul that ended at midnight. Built by the Roman consul somewhere between AD 161 and 174, the Theatre of Herodes is on the southern slope of the Acropolis and seats 5,000 spectators. Having seen televised productions at this outdoor theatre, it seemed a perfect opportunity to do like thousands before me had done — to sit on the same rock-hard seats on a warm summer evening with a million stars overhead.

I found a production of the opera Norma was scheduled for an evening I was in Athens. The hotel staff assured me I could walk to the theatre; that is what most Greeks do. I studied my map, left early, and paid attention to the shops along the way as markers for my return.

As the opera concluded, I followed the crowd along a gravel pathway. Gradually, the crowd thinned. I realized I was walking further rather than closer to my hotel in the Plaka area.

With trepidation I made some turns and found the shops closed that I had counted on to be open. Metal doors were locked down and covered with graffiti.

I cursed myself for being so stupid. There were no taxis to be seen, nor had I seen any outside the theatre. My fast walk became a running walk. I made it to the hotel with a rapidly beating heart.

Being lost is expected in my travels. I do not have a great sense of direction, especially in cities. While wandering the streets, against conventional advice I use my phone to check maps. I move to a place where I am not in the middle of traffic and my back is to the wall of a building. If you are skilled at reading maps and memorizing your path, do it. I am just not able to do so. I need to check along the way.

### The Purse Stays With You---Always

When traveling, it is wise to leave designer handbags and expensive jewelry at home. Difficult as it is to be prepared for every situation — such as rain — it is not easy to abandon the idea of carrying a purse. The advice to keep your handbag close at all times also applies when seated. The back of the chair does not exist for you to hang your purse. In San Francisco, that is how a friend discovered her wallet was missing when leaving a bagel shop. Always have it touching a part of your body, even if you put it between your feet or on your lap.

### When in Rome (or Chelsea), Do as the Locals Do

Blending into the environment reduces your risk of being tagged as a wealthy tourist just begging to be departed from her valuables. Learn cultural customs of the country and dress in a conservative fashion. Strolling along a street in Chelsea, I was stopped by a well-dressed woman and asked how I was going to vote on the Council Tax. Of course, the minute I opened my mouth it was apparent I was not a Londoner. However, I took pride in the fact I was blending in.

Traveling in Spain with her three teenagers who were bilingual, a friend instructed them to only speak Spanish so they would not be identified as U.S. tourists.

### Social Lies That Save

When conversing with others and your gut tells you to be careful, here are some ploys I have used.

- Give only your middle name when asked for your name.
- Say you are leaving the next day.
- Your boyfriend is waiting for you back at the hotel.

- I have a local boyfriend, and he would not like me seeing you; he is the jealous type.
- You already have plans for the evening or whenever they are suggesting.
- "Where's your significant other?" Respond with "Where is your wife?"
- I have a ring that could be a wedding band and wear it in places where males are more aggressive.

## Grand Bazaar, Grand Escape

On a hot muggy Istanbul day in July, I decided to lose myself in the Grand Bazaar. Very few merchants had enclosed and air-conditioned stalls. Pausing to get a closer look at a lambskin jacket cut in an unusual style, I caught the attention of the merchant. Leaving the comfort of his air conditioned "cage," he approached encouraging me to "come inside" and try the jacket on. Caving, I welcomed the coolness of the room and tried on the jacket. I loved it! "Cost to you, special," he said. I knew then it would be exorbitant. He stated a price. Shocked, I protested that I was a poor professor and could not afford such a luxury. I continued to protest at each subsequent price. After several rounds of haggling, he eventually came down to 5,000 Euros. Then he said to me with a gleam in his eye, "I will gift it to you." I tore the jacket off and ran.

It scares me when I tell a woman this story and her response is that she would have taken the jacket as a gift. Nothing is free and one can be sure he would want his pound of flesh. At the very least, I knew what my price was.

# TRAVEL DOCUMENTS

Turkish Visa

*"If he were allowed contact with foreigners, he would discover that they were creatures like himself and that most of what he had been told about them is lies. The sealed world in which he lives would be broken, and the fear, hatred and self-righteousness on which his morale depends might evaporate."* George Orwell, 1984

# CHAPTER 5

## LESSONS FROM THE "READY LANE"

Even when traveling to Mexico, a Passport is required. I knew this. Somewhere deep in the recesses of my mind, I knew this. And yet, there I was, inching forward in a never-ending line at the U.S./Mexico border, utterly passport-less, sweat dripping down my back. (Because I am so sweaty I am fearful the border guard will think I am attempting to smuggle drugs across the border.)

It had been a few years since I'd last visited Mexico, back when a driver's license could suffice for border crossings. Unfortunately, 2011 changed all that and I was apparently still stuck in a pre-passport reality. As the cars around me crept forward bumper to bumper, with no escape route in sight, I began a slow descent into panic. The blinking red light ahead read *"Ready Lane."* I had no idea what that meant, but I was not ready for anything, except to get across the border and home.

When I finally reached the booth, the stern CBP agent —

young, uniformed and accessorized with an intimidating belt of weapons — greeted me with a rapid-fire interrogation.

"Your pass card, please," he barked.

"Oh...I don't have one," I stammered, my heart racing.

"Your Passport, then?"

"I forgot it at home."

I might as well have confessed to plotting world domination. The scolding that followed could have made a hardened criminal weep. He demanded my driver's license and disappeared into his booth for what felt like a small eternity, leaving me to stew in a cocktail of shame, regret and fear of being denied entry to the United States.

When he finally returned, he interrogated me further: "What are you bringing back? Why did you go to Mexico? How long were you there? Open the trunk!"

These were familiar questions. I'd heard them before and oddly, they offered some comfort. Maybe, just maybe, I'd escape this ordeal with my freedom intact. After a final glare and a stern warning about leaving the country without proper documentation, he handed me my driver's license and waved me through. I wanted to hit the gas and vanish into the distance, but I resisted the urge. No need to tempt fate further.

## PASSPORTS: YOUR GOLDEN TICKET

The moral of this story? Always, always bring your Passport. Unlike traveling domestically, where a driver's license is usually sufficient, international travel demands this magical little booklet. It's not just a formality — it's your golden ticket to cross borders, avoid sticky situations and generally not end up in a bureaucratic mess.

If you're anything like me, you probably keep your Passport in a "safe place," which is great until you forget where that place is. So, here's some advice: Keep it in a spot where you'll always remember, like your travel bag. And make sure it's current. Check that you have enough blank pages and that it doesn't expire within six months of your return date. Some countries are sticklers for this rule, and you don't want to be denied entry because of an overlooked expiration date.

## COPIES AND BACKUPS BECAUSE MURPHY'S LAW EXISTS

Traveling with just one copy of your passport is like playing roulette with your sanity. Be smart — scan the main page (the one with your charming photo) and upload it to the Cloud. Email a copy to yourself, stash printed copies in your luggage and even snap a photo on your smartphone. Why? Because losing your passport mid-trip is the travel equivalent of a horror movie and having backups can make the whole ordeal slightly less terrifying.

If you do lose it, the local U.S. Embassy is your lifeline. Pro tip: Look up the embassy's address before you go and save it in your contacts and itinerary. You'll thank yourself later.

## TRAVEL QUIRKS: CRUISES

Cruise ships have their own quirks. Some hold onto passengers' passports for the duration of the trip, which sounds terrifying until you realize your cabin keycard acts as your temporary ID. The first time this happened, I spent two days nervously imagining myself stranded in a foreign port. Thankfully, I never had to test the keycard theory.

## THE EVOLUTION OF BORDER CONTROL: BIOMETRICS AND ETIAS

In Europe, passport control is evolving faster than I can keep up. Since November 2024, biometric passports with embedded chips allow you to breeze through self-service kiosks at EU borders — when the technology cooperates, of course.

But starting in 2025, the EU introduced ETIAS (European Travel Information and Authorization System). If you're from a visa-exempt country, you'll need to apply for this travel authorization online before entering the EU or Britain. It's valid for three years or until your passport expires, whichever comes first. The good news? If you're over 70, the application fee is waived. Finally, a senior perk worth celebrating!

## VISAS: THE HIDDEN HURDLE

Ah, visas. Some countries make it easy, letting you buy one at the airport upon arrival. Others, like Cuba, require advance planning. Egypt's visa can be obtained online. Then there's Russia, which takes bureaucracy to an Olympic level.

When I applied for a Russian visa, I had to fill out forms that asked everything short of my childhood pet's name. They wanted to know my grade school, my employers and the exact dates of my trips over the past decade. To top it off, I needed proof of hotel reservations and an official invitation letter. Last step in the process is the approval of the Russian Embassy.

I refused to entrust my precious passport to a third party. Instead, I personally delivered it to the Russian Embassy in Washington, D.C. Call me paranoid, but the thought of my passport floating around in a stranger's hands gave me heart palpitations.

**LESSONS LEARNED: DOCUMENTS FIRST, FUN LATER**

Traveling is exhilarating, but it's also a game of preparation. Your Passport? That's your MVP — your best friend, lifeline and ticket to adventure. Treat it with care, back it up, and always know where it is. Whether you're crossing a land border or jetting off to Paris, having the right documents can save you from unnecessary stress (and a scolding from a border agent).

So, double-check your Passport, organize your visas, and set yourself up for smooth travels. Once that's done, you're free to focus on the fun part: booking flights, planning escapades, and soaking up new experiences. Just one final pro tip: the Ready Lane is not your friend if you're not actually *ready*. Trust me on this one.

# ACCESSIBILITY WHEN TRAVELING

*Cobblestone Street in Ghent, Belgium*

*"Let's stop 'tolerating' or 'accepting' difference, as if we're so much better for not being different in the first place. Instead, let's celebrate difference, because in this world it takes a lot of guts to be different." Kate Bornstein*

# CHAPTER 6

## Overcoming Challenges and Embracing Adventures

As the years pile on, our bodies sometimes start to wage small, silent protests. Knees creak like an old staircase, stairs feel like they've multiplied overnight, and even our hearing and vision might decide to take occasional coffee breaks.

These shifts may be uninvited, but they are no reason to stop exploring the world. With some planning, adaptability and a healthy sense of humor, the joys of travel remain as vibrant as ever — whether you're trekking through ancient ruins or navigating a modern airport.

### Facing Accessibility Challenges: A Tale of Two Perspectives

When pondering the spectrum of accessibility in travel, I'm reminded of two starkly different experiences. In St. Petersburg, Russia, I once asked about options for travelers with mobility issues. The reply was an unapologetic, "They just stay home." It was like being smacked with a cold, hard truth about how some places still treat accessibility as an afterthought — or worse, ignore it entirely.

Contrast that with the memory of a 90-year-old gentleman from the Czech Republic I met on a private tour in Cappadocia, Turkey. Watching him effortlessly maneuver the winding, uneven paths of ancient caves, squeezing through one cave to another, made me question all my excuses. He was agile, confident and radiated a zest for life that made me realize age isn't the deciding factor for adventure — it's attitude. Sure, some physical limitations are non-negotiable, but how we adapt to them is what truly matters.

A SURPRISING REVELATION: **Cabo San Lucas**

Cabo San Lucas in Mexico turned out to be a delightful surprise in the world of accessible travel. When a friend joined me there, arriving unexpectedly in a wheelchair, I initially panicked. My mind raced through potential roadblocks: uneven terrain, inaccessible hotels, a lack of ramps. I envisioned a week filled with awkward improvisation and limited movement.

To my astonishment, Cabo proved to be one of the most accessible destinations I've ever visited. Sidewalks sloped gently where I expected treacherous steps. Ramps appeared at every corner and even the hotel where we stayed seemed designed with accessibility in mind. My friend transitioned from her wheelchair to a foldable knee scooter after landing and suddenly, the world felt open to us again.

From beachfront strolls to bustling markets, Cabo didn't just accommodate our needs — it excelled at them. It was a masterclass in how thoughtful design can turn potential obstacles into non-issues. It reminded me that accessibility isn't just about convenience; it's about inclusion and the freedom to explore.

### The Power of Asking for Help

If there's one golden rule for navigating travel challenges, it's this: Never be afraid to ask for help. Whether it's a wheelchair at the airport, assistance with luggage or directions in an unfamiliar city, asking isn't a sign of weakness — it's a savvy traveler's secret weapon.

Airports can be endurance tests masquerading as transit hubs. Terminals can stretch for what feels like miles. By the time you reach Gate 37 you might feel like you've run a marathon. Before my knee surgery, I regularly requested a wheelchair for these long treks. Initially, I hesitated — there's something about asking for help that can feel a little uncomfortable. But after navigating a few sprawling terminals, I quickly learned the value of conserving energy for the actual journey.

One memorable experience involved a young airport attendant who seemed to believe he was competing in a race, zooming me through the expansive terminal with such speed my friend had to jog to keep up.

Pro tip: Be responsible in using these services. Early boarding might seem like an enticing perk, but wheelchairs and assistance should be reserved for those who genuinely need them. And if you do need them, don't hesitate — that's what they're there for. Do tip wheelchair assistants; they only receive the numeration from tips. They are not airport employees.

. . .

EUROPE'S ACCESSIBILITY: **Beauty Meets Frustration**

Europe is a dream destination for many, with its rich history, stunning architecture and romantic landscapes. But for travelers with mobility concerns, it can sometimes feel like a mixed bag.

Take the Paris Metro, for example. It's iconic, but let's be honest — it's more stairs than subway. Boarding times are short, and elevators are rarer than an uncrowded photo of the Eiffel Tower. Then there are the cobblestone streets, which look charming in photos but are a nightmare for wheels and unsteady walkers alike.

The solution? Plan. Plan. Plan. Research accessible routes, find out which train stations have elevators and prepare for a few inevitable hurdles. Many European cities are making strides in accessibility, but progress can be uneven, so a little extra preparation goes a long way.

NAVIGATING **Hearing Loss While Traveling**

Traveling with hearing loss presents its own unique set of challenges. I've traveled with companions who struggled to hear announcements in noisy airports, communicate with hotel staff, or follow group tours. It can be frustrating, not to mention isolating, when conversations or instructions are missed.

Preparation is key: Ensure hearing aids are in good working condition and pack extra batteries. You don't want to be halfway through a walking tour only to realize you're out of power. Consider downloading apps that transcribe speech or amplify sound; they can be lifesavers in noisy environments. Clear communication isn't just convenient — it's essential for a smooth travel experience.

## A Glimpse into Visual Impairment

Though I have full vision, there have been moments that gave me a newfound appreciation for the challenges faced by travelers with visual impairments. Whether it was trying to decipher a train schedule in a language I couldn't read or stumbling through a low-light museum display, I've had brief glimpses of how disorienting it can be to navigate the world without full visual clarity. Kafka's museum in Prague is a shining example how disoriented one can be in such low light. I know it was intentional, but how does someone with low vision experience the displays?

For visually impaired travelers, accessibility can mean anything from braille signage to audio navigation tools. These resources aren't universally available, so research is crucial. Finding apps or services that provide real-time navigation assistance can make a significant difference in unfamiliar places.

## The Bigger Picture: Accessibility is a Journey

Accessibility in travel isn't just about physical accommodations. It's about creating spaces and experiences that welcome everyone. While some destinations excel in this area, others still have a long way to go. The key is to approach each trip with curiosity, flexibility and a willingness to adapt.

Every challenge you face on the road is an opportunity to learn, grow, and — let's be honest — collect some entertaining stories to share later. Whether you're inspired by a 90-year-old trekking through Turkish caves or simply relieved to find a ramp when you need one, the world is still full of possibilities.

Keep exploring, embrace the bumps along the way, and remember: A great adventure is often less about where you go and more about how you get there.

# AIR TRANSPORTATION

*Airport St. Petersburg, Russia*

"Once you have tasted flight, you will forever walk the earth with your eyes turned skyward. For there you have been, and there you will always long to return." Leonardo da Vinci.

# CHAPTER 7

### Transportation: A Personal Perspective

When planning a trip, two big-ticket items always top the budget: transportation and lodging. Once I've penciled in potential travel dates, reservations become my immediate focus. Unless there's a compelling reason to stick to specific dates, I like to keep things flexible. Being able to adjust often unlocks better deals.

Now, when it comes to booking flights, the age-old debate continues: book early or wait for last-minute bargains? Some swear by the thrill of chasing down those elusive specials, but me? I'm Team Book Early. My sanity doesn't enjoy the suspense of gambling on airfare roulette.

### Working with an Agent? Do Your Homework First

If you're considering using a third-party booking service, my advice is to first do reconnaissance yourself. Get a sense of airfare ranges for your dates and destinations. Personally,

I often work with a consolidator, but I make my preferences crystal clear:

- Preferred airlines (and those I wouldn't touch with a 10-foot boarding pass).
- Ideal departure and arrival times.
- A firm request to avoid switching airlines mid-journey.
- If a layover is unavoidable, I insist on at least 90 minutes even when staying with the same airline.
- Major airports can be sprawling and running from one end of the terminal to the other isn't my idea of pre-flight cardio. This is when you might consider asking for assistance.

### Timing Your Arrival

For safety and sanity, I aim to arrive at new destinations during daylight hours. Familiar places? That's another story. I've had my share of late-night arrivals: Alaska at midnight (bright as day in summer), Dubai in the wee hours (manageable, but disorienting), and Venice close to midnight (a logistical headache I don't care to repeat). The lesson? Prioritize arrival times unless you enjoy nocturnal adventures.

### The Case for Comfort Over Coach

Age has its perks, including the wisdom to prioritize comfort. My rule is simple: if the flight is longer than six hours, business class is non-negotiable. If I can't afford it, the trip waits. It's a personal and financial choice, but for me, sleep is sacred, and a flatbed seat is the throne of in-flight comfort. Jet lag also hits differently when you've had a proper rest.

Domestic business class rarely includes lie-flat seats, but international flights often do. On many trips, I fly business class across the ocean but I tend to opt for economy within the destination countries — a compromise that keeps costs in check without sacrificing sleep.

### Navigating the Friendly Skies

Flying business class comes with some perks that make the experience far more pleasant — like amenity kits filled with toothpaste, toothbrush, eye mask, socks, lip balm and a small container of moisturizer. If you are lucky enough to snag one, don't bother packing those items yourself. Instead, save your carry-on space for the real essentials, like a good book or something to binge watch, medicines, and reading glasses.

Now, let's address the in-flight climate: The air is drier than the desert on a bad day. Pack moisturizer for your hands and face, along with eye drops. And do your eyeballs a favor — ditch the contact lenses. Wear your glasses on the plane and put your lenses in after you land. Pro tip: Skip the first restroom in the terminal after landing. Everyone else will swarm there and the next one is usually quieter and cleaner.

### The Airport Gauntlet

First stop at the airport: check-in. If you haven't done this online, head to the counter or your airline's kiosk. If you are checking luggage, it's often cheaper to prepay online than to pay at the airport. Or check at the curb before entering the terminal.

Next up: security. TSA's rules are unpredictable. To speed things up, make sure you've reviewed TSA's guidelines ahead of time. The liquid rules are notoriously tricky — did you know that toothpaste counts as a liquid? Neither did I until an overzealous agent confiscated mine.

If you are enrolled in TSA Pre-check, congratulations — you get to skip the hassle of removing shoes, laptops, belts and your neatly packed quart bag of toiletries. Just make sure your Known Traveler Number (KTN) is attached to your reservation, or you will end up in the regular security line with the rest of us mere mortals. Pro Tip: Place all loose items in your carry on or purse instead of placing them in the basket that goes through the scanner. The basket has held how many shoes before you?

### Titanium Knees and TSA Drama

For those of us with body implants (hello, titanium knees) you will need to alert the first TSA agent you see that you require a full-body scan. If you forget, you will set off the scanner and be treated to the delightful experience of a full-body pat down. I have been there — it was educational. While you can request a private screening, I personally opt for the public pat down —it is faster, and frankly, I'm not sure anyone at TSA has the time or inclination to make it awkward. I will ask for a male next time.

\* \* \*

## Lounges: **Luxury or Letdown?**

Business and first-class tickets usually come with lounge access — a quiet refuge while you wait to board. Well, quiet is relative. These days, lounges are busier, nosier and more crowded than they used to be. Sometimes they even run out of space entirely and the hours they are available have diminished. Food options have dwindled, and you might have to pay for drinks. Still, lounge agents are a lifesaver if your flight is delayed or cancelled. They are often able to assist you in making the necessary schedule adjustments. Some airports now even offer separate lounges for first-class passengers, so if that's you, enjoy the exclusivity while it lasts.

### Hydration and Snacks

Once you have cleared security, fill up your reusable water bottle. Flight attendants rarely serve enough water to keep you hydrated; you don't want to be that annoying passenger pressing the call button every 30 minutes.

As for snacks, I have a few personal favorites: chocolate, protein bars, nuts, apples, a homemade sandwich and more chocolate. Avoid anything with a strong odor — your fellow passengers don't need to share the olfactory experience of your boiled eggs or tuna salad. Careful with your choice of cheeses. You might be evicted from the plane if you bring Epoisse, one of the top 10 stinkiest cheeses in the world.

### To Pack **or Not to Pack: A Change of Clothes**

Many travel advisors swear by packing a change of clothes in your carry-on in case your luggage goes AWOL.

Me? I've never done it. If disaster strikes, I'll buy something at my destination. Besides, shopping for clothes doubles as a souvenir hunt — and you will always remember the shirt you bought out of necessity in Brisbane or Tangier.

### Dress Smart, Travel Smart

When it comes to in-flight fashion, comfort reigns supreme. Loose clothing, compression socks and closed-toed shoes are non-negotiable. Airplane cabins can get chilly, so pack a jacket or pashmina scarf.

While comfort is key, I draw the line at outfits that belong exclusively at home. Like it or not, people — including flight staff — respond to how you present yourself. A little effort can go a long way.

### Survival Kit for Coach Class

Flying economy? Here is your list of must-haves to make the journey bearable:

- Toothbrush and toothpaste
- Snacks (non-smelly, of course)
- Refillable water bottle
- Lip balm, moisturizer and eye drops
- Reading material or an e-reader
- Neck pillow, eye mask and noise-cancelling headphones
- A pen for filling out customs forms
- Your prescription medications
- Reading glasses

With these in tow, even the longest flights can feel (almost) manageable.

**RE-ENTRY: Global Entry Makes it Easy**

Returning to the U.S.? Global Entry is your best friend. After passport control, you simply pop your global entry card into a kiosk, answer a few questions, and voila — you are on your way to baggage claim, breezing past customs. It is a game-changer. Applying online is straightforward, though it does require an in-person interview. The card is valid for five years, and trust me, it's worth every penny.

## FINAL THOUGHTS

Traveling is an adventure, but it's also a lesson in preparation and adaptability. Whether you are in first class or the back of the plane, a little foresight goes a long way in making the journey enjoyable. Trust me, a little extra thought about transportation can turn a good trip into a great one — or at least spare you from airport sprints and midnight misadventures.

# LODGING

*Lodge at Victoria Falls, Zimbabwe*

"I stayed in a really old hotel last night. They sent me a wake-up letter." Steven Wright, comedian

# CHAPTER 8

**Securing Lodging**

For me, securing lodging the first night of arrival is second only to flight reservations. Not knowing where I will be resting my head each night is outside of my comfort zone. There's something about not knowing where I'll be sleeping that just doesn't sit well with me anymore. I used to thrive on that kind of uncertainty in my 20s — sometimes even found it thrilling. But as time has passed, my desire for a solid, confirmed bed has grown. These days, I sometimes book my last night in a hotel near the airport. It's a win-win: I can calmly lay out everything, pack with no panic and get a bit more sleep without stressing about timeliness of booked airport transportation. In Miami, before heading to Cuba, I used the extra time to chat with fellow travelers about our varied approaches to booking hotels, comparing tips like we were all part of some secret club.

\* \* \*

## Booking Strategy

One thing I proudly explained to my fellow Cuba travelers is my multiple-booking technique. I use several sources to book my accommodations, always ensuring that cancellations are free up to a certain date. This way, I can make overlapping bookings at different hotels in different parts of the city, which gives me the freedom to make the final decision a month out after checking the maps, reviews, and websites. For example, in Paris, I've booked hotels in various arrondissements to explore different corners of the city in depth.

## Types of Lodging

From chain hotels to boutique stays, hostels (which I still haven't been brave enough to try), Bed and Breakfasts, Airbnb's and even glamping — I've tested most options. I've been told elderly hostels are the budget choice for mature travelers, but I think I'll pass on that adventure for now.

## Booking Criteria

When it comes to booking, here's what I look for:

- A location near something I'll want to visit, like a museum or transportation hub.
- Breakfast included or a nearby café that I can stumble into in my morning haze.
- A flexible cancellation policy (because plans can change, and I like my options).
- A budget base and a maximum — got to keep it realistic.

- 24-hour front desk, because who knows when a late-night snack or some extra shampoo will be needed? I consider this a safety item
- Amenities like Wi-Fi (obviously).
- A rooftop bar or café (major bonus points).
- A centrally located spot, so I can pop back in for a nap if I overdo it with sightseeing.
- Transportation to and from the airport — because that's never as easy as it should be.

These were my guidelines when booking the hotel in Mexico City that gave my injured friend the VIP treatment.

### Negotiating **Rates**

Sometimes calling the hotel directly can work in your favor too. A polite "Can you offer a better rate?" can work wonders. I've also tried the "It's my special occasion" trick to get some extra perks. Let's just say it's been less successful than I'd hoped — more likely to earn me a raised eyebrow than an upgrade.

### Room inspection

Before unpacking, I do a quick room inspection. I check cleanliness, waste baskets, bed presentation and the quirks of the heating system or unusual light switches. I avoid rooms near elevators — those late-night partyers and the elevator itself are often noisier than they seem. I also steer clear of rooms near ice machines. And having no window — or one that faces a wall — is a definite deal-breaker. Ground floor? Not a chance. Remember, I had my cash stolen while sitting by the pool in Montego Bay once and I'm not repeating that mistake.

Travel advisors often recommend booking your room on floors three to six — a sweet spot, they say, for safety and practicality. It's high enough to avoid any unexpected late-night window visitors (unless Spider-Man is on your travel itinerary), but low enough that in the unlikely event of an emergency, you're not left contemplating how many fire drills you slept through in high school.

It's also a personal preference of mine. Sure, penthouse views are lovely, but I've always felt more secure knowing I'm just a few flights away from solid ground. Besides, who wants to wait 15 minutes for an elevator that insists on stopping at every floor when you could be halfway down the stairs and already planning your next adventure?

### Concierge Tips

Hotel concierges are the unsung heroes of travel. They know the ins and outs, from restaurants to tours to hard-to-get theater tickets. And yes, they do appreciate tips — especially when you're asking them to pull off something difficult, like getting a dinner reservation at a popular spot or a theatre ticket to a "sold out" show.

### Settling into a Routine

If you're staying in one place for a few days, settle into a routine. Find a local café or bar nearby where the staff gets to know you. In Athens, I made it a point to work at a café close to my hotel each day, nursing a glass of wine in "my corner". After a few days, they were topping up my glass without even asking. They became my unofficial tour guides, sharing tips and advice I wouldn't have found in any guidebook.

### Essential Hotel Card

Always take the hotel business card when you check in. Pop it into your contact list and make sure you have the hotel name and address written out in the local script, whether it's Cyrillic, Arabic, Chinese, or Japanese. If you get lost or need a cab, you'll be glad you have it.

### Lessons in Problem Solving

Even when you do all the right things, you will encounter situations that test your problem-solving skills. The importance of having the hotel phone number and address was impressed upon me when friends and I arrived in Bali.

Our "home" was a trilevel in Ubud, an area of Bali known as the monkey forest. The first floor was up a set of stairs and had its own balcony along two sides of the house. Our first evening we settled in with drinks and snacks out on the balcony. As the evening wore on, one of the women went back into the house for more wine. She closed the door as she returned to the balcony. Soon, we discovered we were locked out. All of us had cell phones, so our first instinct was to call the front desk for assistance. Problem was, we did not know the number, so we needed to look it up on the Internet.

Unfortunately, the signal was not strong enough to access the Internet. We were down a long walkway from the reception area so we thought perhaps if we yelled loud enough help would find its way to us. By this time, it was dark, our throats were sore, and our voices were becoming hoarse. Only the monkeys heard us.

We paced about looking for possibilities. Two of us, wearing long flowing light-weight summer dresses decided we could tie our dresses together and go down to the ground like in the movies. Meanwhile one of our travel companions was getting hysterical adding to the tension. We decided against this plan.

Our next idea was to break the glass in the door and reach around for the handle. The search was on for a tool. We settled on a chair and one of us banged the door with it, unsuccessfully. It then was my turn so I considered physics and decided that maybe it would work were I to put the force of my whole body into the attack on the glass. Bingo! It worked.

The next day we looked at where we would have landed had we tried the dresses idea and realized we could have been seriously injured. That afternoon the door was repaired. When we asked about it we were told it happens all the time. When checking out we found no charge on our bill for the repairs.

My lodging experiences are as varied as the cities I've visited — Airbnb's, B&Bs, glam tents, VRBO, friends' homes, big chain hotels, boutique gems, and yes, even a college dormitory. But if I'm being honest, my heart belongs to the small, locally-owned boutique hotels, Bed & Breakfasts and glam tents (only in Africa). When I travel, the last thing I want to do is wash dishes, make the bed or scrub the toilet. I prefer to leave all that to someone else. I am on vacation after all.

I'm also not keen on meeting strangers just to rent a

room in their home. While I'm all for adventure, I like the idea of returning to a comfortable, secure place at the end of the day, not wondering if the locks on the door work. That rules out a few of the more budget-friendly options.

For example, I booked a VRBO rental in Kyrenia, Cyprus. I thought I'd done my due diligence. Turns out, not well enough. When I arrived, I was so disturbed by the place that I didn't even want to open my luggage. The front door didn't close properly, there were missing light bulbs, and the TV was a tiny, ancient black-and-white relic. But the real winners were the filthy bathroom and kitchen and the dim, somewhat ominous stairwell leading up to the unit. Oh, and did I mention the two-story pile of garbage outside the building? I was terrified to stay there.

I called the company to complain, but apparently, an entry door that did not close properly, missing light bulbs and a pile of garbage weren't "valid" complaints. They assured me these were just minor repairs the local representative (an hour away, mind you) could handle. I checked into a hotel instead and never saw a penny of my money again. Lesson learned: I won't take a risk on VRBO or Airbnb's again unless I know the owner personally — or, in some cases, even then. But hey, you may have had better luck with these budget-friendly options. If they work for you, more power to you.

Airbnb's have certainly shaken up the lodging industry over the past few years, and not in a small way. It's even caught the attention of hotel chains and local governments. Several popular cities, including Barcelona, Venice, Paris, and San Francisco, have started putting the brakes on the number of licenses they issue to Airbnb hosts, limiting how many units can be rented out. It's not just to control the sheer number of tourists (though, let's face it, that's part of it); it's also about preserving neighborhood integrity and, perhaps more importantly, addressing the housing crisis by freeing up rentals for locals. So, while Airbnb's might be a godsend for some, it seems that in certain places, it's no longer easy to find one.

## BATHROOMS

When it comes to travel, the range of "personal accommodations" is as varied as the places you'll visit. Some days you might find yourself mastering the art of squatting over a hole (trust me, those squats come in handy), with a bucket of water nearby to flush — or, if you're lucky, a nice, clean, modern bathroom with familiar features, perhaps even segregated by gender. Oh, and don't forget the occasional trip behind a bush (a real "nature call").

The names for these necessary facilities are equally diverse. You'll encounter loos, water closets, happy rooms, lavatories, bathrooms, powder rooms, los baños, restrooms, ladies' rooms and the ever-elusive "necessary room." I always get a small chuckle when I ask, "Where's the happy room?" A memorable experience occurred in Cienfuegos, Cuba, where the hotel desk clerk refused to tell me where "los baños" were until I could properly pronounce "los baños." It took me at least a dozen attempts before he finally relented. Was he messing with me? Probably.

Here's my most crucial travel tip: always carry toilet paper. You never know when you'll be caught in a situation where it's not provided — and when it is, it might come in the form of a single square at a time. Sometimes, there's even a small fee for the privilege. So, pack wisely and don't take the risk of being caught unprepared.

## Other Accommodations

The strangest facility I found was in an upscale restaurant in Brussels, the Belga Queen. It was unisex and everyone washed their hands and dried them with thick cloths at a rectangular communal sink in the center of the room. On the periphery were stalls with glass doors enabling you to see if occupied. I observed one person sitting down and then once the door closed realized she could be seen by everyone, got up and bolted out.

Curious me decided there must be a trick to this translucent door. Too many people were entering and leaving but not distressed. There had to be some way to make the glass opaque while sitting or standing there. So, I went in, looked for a switch but nothing obvious. A little patience was needed. I fiddled with the door handle and discovered a button below the handle which I pushed. Voila! That not only locked the door, but it turned the glass opaque, providing the essential privacy.

When it comes to choosing lodging, the options are endless, and each stay brings a new set of decisions. Personally, I lean toward places that offer a little more local character, something that feels like it truly belongs in the destination. Chain hotels are fine if you just need the basics, but honestly, they could be anywhere.

Do I have a favorite hotel? Oh, absolutely. A music-themed hotel in Prague with a rooftop restaurant and bar? Yes, please. If I had to live in a hotel (let's be real, that would be a dream), this would be it. It even has a secret door leading to an adjacent baroque garden and Charles Bridge is nearby. The rooms are beautifully decorated, comfy and the staff is friendly. It's my version of "hotel perfection."

When I stay in Cabo San Lucas, I opt for a spot on the marina, within walking distance of everything downtown. Some people might call it "old and in need of an update," but to me it's the perfect balance of location and local charm. All-inclusive resorts? Not my thing. They're the same in Jamaica or Mexico and pretty much everywhere else. While that may be comforting for some, I'd rather explore the local restaurants and soak up the culture.

In the end, lodging takes up a good chunk of your travel budget, and it impacts your experience. Your choice comes down to your own preferences: Sometimes you want a specific vibe and sometimes you're just looking for the essentials. But no matter what, your home away from home should make you feel comfortable enough to rest up for the adventures ahead.

# FOOD

*Wine and Cheese*

*"When you travel, remember that a foreign country is not designed to make you comfortable. It is designed to make its own people comfortable." Clifton Fediman*

# CHAPTER 9

Over the years, I've come to realize breakfast is the unsung hero of travel days. A good, hearty breakfast sets the tone and fuels me for hours of exploration, wandering and the inevitable wrong turns.

Hotel breakfast buffets are my go-to. They're convenient, varied and often so generous that I can coast through the day without needing lunch. Pro tip: Keep a zip-lock bag handy. Many buffets offer fruit or nuts that can be discreetly pocketed for snacking later. At a hotel in Istanbul, the breakfast spread was so satisfying that I happily skipped lunch, especially with a few delicious, dried apricots tucked away for an afternoon pick-me-up.

Of course, there's something magical about stepping out to a local café for breakfast. Beginning a morning with coffee and a buttery croissant while watching the world wake up around you is an experience I treasure. Cities like Brussels and Paris are perfect for this. There's nothing quite like soaking up the charm of a bustling square as the locals go about their day.

. . .

**SNACKS AND STREET FOOD: The Thrill and the Risk**

Street food is an exciting part of travel. It's spontaneous, it's local and always comes with a story. But let me add a word of caution: street food isn't for everyone. If your stomach isn't adventurous or you have a compromised immune system, it's best to admire from a distance, no matter how tempting the aromas might be.

That said, some cities make street food an irresistible adventure. In Istanbul I was surprised to see that the most popular options were corn on the cob and Simits, pretzel-like bread. Another favorite is Dondurma, which often comes with a lively performance by the ice cream vendor. In Brussels, waffles and pommes frites are almost impossible to resist — they practically call out to you from the carts. And in Mexico, my go-to street snacks are fresh fruit and tacos, bursting with flavor.

**ROOM SERVICE: A Quiet Respite**

There's something inherently luxurious about room service, isn't there? The idea of food arriving on a tray, just for you, is hard to resist. While I try not to rely on it too often — because it means missing out on local food and culture — it can be a lifesaver when you're too exhausted to head out or just need a little peace and quiet.

For those early mornings with tight schedules, room service has been my best friend. It's a relief to know that I can eat quickly and without hassle, saving precious minutes for catching a flight or starting a tour. It's also a good option when I need to be alone with my thoughts — or my pajamas.

. . .

**FROM AWKWARD to Empowered**

Eating alone can feel daunting at first. I've had my fair share of awkward moments, like being seated by the door, next to the kitchen, or in some shadowy corner that seems designed to hide me from view. These days, I've learned to politely request a better table — or, if necessary, move myself.

Barcelona provided one of my more memorable solo dining experiences. In a very crowded restaurant, I was ushered to the bar after attempting to sit at a table for six, much to the amusement of everyone around me. The waiter and I didn't share a common language, but that didn't stop us from putting on a comical show of hand gestures and raised eyebrows. By the end of the charades I was, for a moment, part of the entertainment.

To make solo dining more enjoyable, I've developed a few strategies. Bringing a book or notebook is always helpful. Writing about the day or observing the people around me keeps my mind occupied. Once, while jotting down notes by the Bosporus, I glanced up to find a videographer filming me. Apparently, "solo writer by the water" was the aesthetic they were looking for.

At a hotel breakfast I found all the tables taken, some for four with only one person seated at them. About to ask staff to open another section, I told myself to be brave and ask someone if I could join them. The worst answer would be "no" and I could move on. The first person I asked was a woman at a table for six. She welcomed me and regaled me with tales of travel, making my breakfast a laugh-filled one. I would have liked to continue the conversation, but that is one circumstance of traveling: Meeting people and wanting to maintain contact but knowing it just does not happen all that often.

Ordering food from the bar is often quicker and the menu is the same. I was struck by a couple at Gary Danko's in San Francisco. They were regulars at the bar, engaging the bartender in jovial conversation. At restaurants high in demand and difficult to obtain a reservation, sitting at the bar allows you to enjoy food from the same menu, make conversation with the bartender and have great service.

When I was banished to the bar in Barcelona, the bartender became my ally and rescued me from an obnoxious male who had sat down beside me. Once I finished my food, he handed me my check rather than making me ask for it, allowing me to scoot out the door.

People-watching is another great way to pass the time. In Johannesburg, I enjoyed the theater of nearby tables more than the magazines the waitstaff kindly brought me. In Athens, I eavesdropped on conversations and made up my own stories about the couples dining around me. Were they spies? Were they breaking up or was it a secret tryst? My imagination has turned many a quiet meal into a creative writing exercise.

It has taken me many meals to learn to enjoy eating out and alone. Now there are times I prefer it. In Copenhagen, I ordered from a tasting menu. When the waiter brought the dish, time was spent explaining to me the ingredients and how it was prepared. Had I been with someone, it would have been a different experience, especially if that person had limited food choices.

I still remember my very first attempt to dine at a hotel restaurant in Washington D.C. and not be intimidated by being alone. That evening, I noticed a man a few tables away also dining alone staring at me every time my gaze wandered his direction. Finished with my dinner and ordering coffee, I asked the waiter to tell the staring man that should he wish to join me for coffee he was welcome. Excited, he knocked his chair over getting up and then tried to casually saunter over to my table. No memory of the conversation, but I can still envision the look on his face when I got up, said good night without giving my name or room number!

I have booked starred Michelin restaurants on trips and enjoyed every morsel. It was a memorable tasting menu and service, and my seating location did not suffer because I was a solo older woman. Daily specials in many European cafés are often reasonable in price and offer an excellent opportunity to sample the local cuisine.

In the Plaka District of Athens luck was with me. Returning to my hotel to leave literature I had collected, I heard footsteps behind me. A young man insisted I accompany him to a nearby restaurant that he knew about, family-owned and serving exceptional local cuisine. I told him no and went up the stairs to my hotel. Later exiting the hotel, I found him waiting for me. Deciding to accompany him after all, I was wary as I followed him down a narrow side street. He escorted me to a small restaurant. Noticing there was a large table of college girls, I relaxed somewhat. The foods were not familiar to me, so I took what they served at the buffet. The samples of home-cooked Greek dishes were delicious! I felt embarrassed and sad for the owners, seeing people walk in, look at the food, and make faces or some disparaging remark and leave. By being a little braver they could have had a new experience.

Do not be shy about entering a pub for food in Dublin or London. I found one in London that I liked the food enough to return a couple of times. (This may not be true of such establishments in other cultures.) On my last visit the manager said for such a frequent customer he would have to buy me a beer next time. How did he know I was leaving the next morning?

### Adventure Eats

Take advantage of the opportunity to eat foods that may seem exotic to you but everyday food for the residents. Two experiences stand out trying new and unusual foods.

In Buenos Aires I joined a group consisting of friends from Australia, Hungary, Columbia, Scotland and Argentina. There I ate offal, trying everything from lungs, udder, stomach, intestine, tongue, heart, brains and kidney. Watching the Hungarians and Australians making faces and rejecting this delicacy, I was determined to taste everything; at least one bite and perhaps with it covered in chimichurri — a condiment consisting of olive oil, red wine vinegar, garlic, red pepper flakes, finely chopped parsley and dried or fresh oregano.

Another opportunity to enjoy a culture's cuisine was in Scotland where I ate black pudding in addition to the traditional haggis. Black pudding was not new to me as I had a paternal grandmother who made her own, known as blood sausage.

Haggis is basically sheep offal, oatmeal and spices cooked

in the stomach lining of a sheep. It is the center of a celebration of Robert Burns' birthday, called the Burns Supper in late January. Like many other traditional dishes, the flavor varies by the quality of the ingredients and their portions as determined by the chef.

In Australia, I couldn't resist diving into the local cuisine. Kangaroo, alligator, their signature version of pommes frites and the renowned barramundi were all on my menu. Each dish came with its own bit of culinary curiosity and charm — though I couldn't help but wonder if my dinner might hop, slither or swim its way back into my dreams later!

### The Bill: **An Art of Subtlety**

In many countries, particularly in Europe, you'll need to ask for the check. It is not brought to the table until you request it. Do not hold your hand up like in high school and wave it about with vigor. Make eye contact with the waiter and mimic a writing motion.

Tipping customs vary throughout the world. Some places include gratuity in the bill, while others expect only a modest round-up. Always check before leaving extra. Some cultures it is an insult.

### Aisles of Culture **and Curiosity**

Wandering through a grocery store in another country is one of my favorite ways to learn about the local culture. It's like stepping into a mini cultural museum, but with snack samples and produce displays. In cities like Paris, Berlin, Madrid and Stockholm, I've discovered grocers tucked into department store basements, each offering a fascinating peek into local eating habits and daily routines.

Beyond the food, grocery stores are also great for people-watching. Strolling the aisles, I've been just as intrigued by the effortless chic style of local women as I've been by the unfamiliar products on the shelves. It's a mix of anthropology and fashion inspiration — practical and entertaining.

One thing to note: always bring your own bag. Many stores don't provide them. I learned this the hard way in Lisbon when I found myself on the street carrying a peach in one hand and a bottle of port in the other. Let's just say it wasn't my most elegant moment. But now I never leave the hotel without a trusty tote bag tucked away!

**Food, Fun, and Fellowship**

Cooking classes have become a favorite way to immerse myself in a new culture. For solo travelers like me, they're the perfect mix of hands-on learning, local flavors and the opportunity to meet others without the pressure of small talk over a formal dinner. There's something wonderful about bonding over rolling dough or chopping herbs alongside strangers who, by the end of the session, often feel like old friends.

Every class I've taken has left me with more than just recipes. It's given me stories, skills and a deeper appreciation for the local way of life. Take Istanbul, for example. I had the opportunity to help prepare dishes for the hotel restaurant's menu, feeling like a temporary member of the culinary staff. It was a whirlwind of spices, steaming pots and the hum of a busy kitchen, leaving me with a few new tricks and a lot of respect for professional chefs.

Krakow introduced me to the delicate art of pierogi-making. At first, my dumplings were more "abstract sculpture" than food, but by the end, they were passable enough to serve. The joy of sealing dough with a pinch and a prayer while trading laughs with classmates made the experience unforgettable.

In Thailand, things took an unexpected turn when fried ants showed up in my salad. To be fair, the instructor didn't warn us ahead of time — it was more of a "surprise protein" moment. The ants were crunchy, nutty, and, dare I say, not bad. I left the class with a newfound sense of adventure and the realization that my salad repertoire back home was boring.

Then there was Paris, where I squared off with croissant dough in a battle of will and patience. Rolling and folding that buttery pastry was as much a workout as it was an art form. By the end, I wasn't sure whether I was prouder of the golden, flaky results or the fact that I hadn't launched my rolling pin across the kitchen.

Cooking classes don't just teach you how to make a dish — they immerse you in the stories, traditions, and techniques that shape a cuisine. Plus, they're great for the solo traveler who wants to break bread with others without committing to a full-blown group tour. Whether you're folding pierogis, frying ants or wrestling with French pastry, cooking classes remind you that food is as much about connection as it is about sustenance. And if nothing else, they ensure you'll never run out of dinner party anecdotes.

### Final Thoughts

Food is more than just sustenance — it's a sensory

journey into culture, connection and adventure. The fragrance of spices in the air, the bold taste of street food or the unexpected texture of haggis tells a unique story. Whether savoring the familiar or bravely diving into the unfamiliar, each meal invites you to experience the world in new ways. So, grab your fork, embrace the unknown, and let the flavors, aromas and textures of the world surprise you.

# CRUISES

*Windstar off the coast of Costa Rico*

*"Twenty years from now, you will be more disappointed by the things you didn't do than those you did. So, throw off the bowlines. Sail away from safe harbor. Catch the wind in your sails. Explore. Dream. Discover."* H. Jackson Brown, Jr.

# CHAPTER 10

## Cruising: A Solo Traveler's Dream (And a Bit of a Puzzle)

For solo travelers, cruising can feel like a tailor-made adventure. You unpack once, your floating hotel takes care of the logistics, and you wake up each day in a new destination without lifting a finger. It's travel without the "are we there yet?" moments. But before you book that dream cruise, let's wade through the details. Because cruising, my fellow wanderers, is as much about preparation as it is about margaritas on deck.

### The Price of Going It Alone

First, let's address the elephant in the cabin: the single supplement. It's the cruise industry's way of gently (or not so gently) reminding you that life is cheaper in pairs. Depending on the cruise line, you might pay anywhere from 25% to 100% more than the per-person rate. Yes, you read that right — double the cost, just because you prefer a solo adventure.

Some cruise lines now offer single staterooms. These are typically cozy, windowless spaces tucked away like hidden treasure — or, if we're being honest, like Harry Potter's cupboard under the stairs. If you can't imagine spending your evenings in a cabin with all the ambiance of a broom closet, consider springing for a room with a view. Trust me, nothing beats sipping coffee on your private balcony as the sunrise paints the horizon.

### READ THE FINE PRINT, Then Read It Again (Seriously)

Cruises have a knack for looking like incredible bargains — until you realize that the price covers little more than your cabin and basic meals. Want Wi-Fi? That'll cost extra. Prefer a glass of wine with dinner? Prepare for sticker shock. And those Instagram-worthy shore excursions? They might as well come with a "luxury tax."

### CABIN LOCATION

Ah, the great debate of cabin location. Seasoned cruisers swear by midship cabins for their smooth sailing, especially if you're prone to seasickness. I, naturally, booked a forward cabin, thinking I'd enjoy the "ocean views." What I got instead was a masterclass in human pinball every time the ship hit a wave. The cabin on a "barefoot cruise" (more casual) was at the stern next to the engine room. Another mistake as it was next to the engines.

Midship folks? They barely noticed. Next time, I'm

parking myself where the seas are calm — or at least where my balance has a fighting chance.

### SHIP SIZE and Passenger-to-Crew Ratio

Bigger ships come with endless amenities, but they also feel like floating cities where finding your stateroom after dinner is a quest worthy of its own. Smaller ships? Intimate, charming and the crew-to-passenger ratio means you might get a server who knows your coffee order by day two. On the downside, they'll also notice your fourth dessert.

### AMENITIES

Cruise amenities are like a buffet of indulgence. Room service? Dangerous for anyone prone to late-night snack cravings. Spas offer the kind of pampering that could make you forget you're sharing a boat with 3,000 strangers. Fitness centers? Great for working off the 17 croissants you ate at breakfast, but who wants to jog on a treadmill while the ocean jiggles below you? That's advanced cardio.

### DINING OPTIONS and Beverage Packages

Cruise dining is a sport. From all-you-can-eat buffets to swanky specialty restaurants, there's something for everyone. But beverage packages? That's where the math degree comes in handy. "If I drink three cocktails, two lattes, and a glass of wine daily, will I break even?" Spoiler: you will, if only out of sheer determination.

. . .

### Excursions

Excursions are like cruise bingo — some people meticulously pre-book every activity, while others wing it and hope for the best. Whether you're ziplining in the jungle of Costa Rica or simply wandering the local markets, there's always the thrill of discovering something incredible — or realizing you've been charged $30 for a fridge magnet.

### Entertainment and Activities

Cruise entertainment is a glorious mixed bag. You can spend the evening at a Broadway-style show, join a wine-tasting class or attempt bridge with a group of retirees who will crush you. Me? I tried a cooking class and came away with a recipe for a soufflé that collapsed faster than my resolve at the dessert buffet.

### Dress Codes

Formal nights on a cruise are either your time to shine or your time to stress. Some people love the glamour; others wonder why they're trying to pack an entire tuxedo into a carry-on. Personally, I aimed for "beach chic" and ended up somewhere between "resort casual" and "lost tourist."

### Gratuities and Service Charges

Gratuities are automatic on most cruises, which is great because it spares you the awkwardness of figuring out who to tip. However, the moment you see the final service charge, you might wonder if you accidentally adopted half the crew. Worth it, though — they really do deserve it.

TRANSPORTATION **to and from Ports**

Getting to the cruise port is its own mini-adventure. Miss the official shuttle and you're left haggling with a taxi driver who insists it's *just a little further*. After the cruise? The journey back feels like a cruel reminder that your magical floating resort doesn't come with teleportation. Rome comes to mind as one of those ports I will avoid. I had no idea it was such a distance to the city, and in my case, the main railroad station. I did not know about the bus, so obviously I missed it. Alternative was to take a cab for 100 Euros. The train shuttle was only 20 Euros. Last option was to negotiate with a cab driver. After considerable back and forth I managed to get the taxi driver to accept 50 Euros. A little homework would have informed me it is 45 miles to city center from the port. The cost ranges from $5 to $170, depending on the mode of transportation and takes a little over an hour. Needless to say, Rome is not my favorite port.

Before you book, channel your inner detective. Study what's included in the base price and then brace yourself for the add-ons. This is where a spreadsheet becomes your best friend. Yes, it sounds nerdy, but when you're comparing staterooms, excursions, and beverage packages, you'll be grateful for the clarity.

BIG SHIPS, **Small Ships: Finding Your Perfect Fit**

Cruise ships range from intimate vessels carrying 200 passengers to mega-liners hosting over 5,000. Big ships are like floating resorts, complete with ziplines, ice rinks and endless dining options. They're perfect if you thrive on variety and don't mind a crowd.

Smaller ships, however, are a different experience entirely. They often dock closer to ports, making it easier to explore independently. On one smaller cruise, the captain welcomed passengers to the bridge for a Q&A session about navigating the fjords. That level of intimacy is hard to find on a mega-liner where you're more likely to meet the captain only in a pre-recorded safety video.

### DINING: A Feast for the Social and the Solo

One of the joys of cruising is the food. You'll find everything from casual buffets to fine dining experiences that rival Michelin-starred restaurants. If you're traveling solo, dining can be as social — or as solitary — as you like. Open dining options let you choose between sharing a table with other travelers or enjoying a quiet meal alone.

I've had some of my most memorable conversations over dinner with strangers on cruises. There's a special camaraderie among travelers when swapping stories about misadventures ashore or life back home. And if you'd rather not make small talk? Room service and a glass of wine on your balcony are a perfect alternative.

### SEASICKNESS: Don't Let It Ruin Your Voyage

What began as a breezy day trip from San Diego to Ensenada quickly turned into a high-stakes episode of *Extreme Balance Challenges*. Halfway there, the waters decided to throw a tantrum. Plates slid off tables, drinks spilled like a bad comedy gag and simply staying upright became an Olympic event.

At one point, I tried holding onto furniture, only to realize the *bolted-down* stuff wasn't as stable as advertised. The nausea hit with a vengeance, and soon enough, I was doing my best impersonation of a seasick extra in *Titanic*.

Somehow, I made it through, clutching a ginger candy as if it were a life preserver. By the time we docked in Ensenada, the ground felt suspiciously steady — almost smug, like it knew I'd never take it for granted again.

If the idea of feeling queasy at sea has you second-guessing your trip, don't worry. Larger ships are generally more stable and modern stabilizers make even choppy waters manageable. That said, if you're prone to motion sickness, consider booking a cabin midship on a lower deck, where movement is minimal.

Pack motion sickness remedies, whether it's medication, acupressure bands or good old ginger candies. And remember, river cruises and calmer waters, like the Mediterranean, are less likely to trigger seasickness. Just avoid booking a tiny yacht in the open Atlantic unless you enjoy testing your limits.

**The Alcohol Package: To Drink or Not to Drink?**

Drink packages promise unlimited cocktails but read the fine print. Most exclude premium liquors and wines, and some limit when and where you can indulge. Personally, I prefer a pay-as-you-go approach. It's easier on the wallet (and the liver) and I love savoring a nightcap on my balcony without worrying if I've "gotten my money's worth."

. . .

## Organized Fun vs. Independent Wandering

Shore excursions are one of the highlights of cruising, but they can also be pricey. While ship-organized tours are convenient, I often prefer exploring ports independently. There's something magical about strolling the streets of Zadar and discovering the sea organ of Croatia at your own pace. If you do venture out solo, watch the time. Cruise ships don't wait for latecomers and missing the boat (literally) can turn an inexpensive afternoon into a costly adventure.

## Your Home at Sea

When it comes to cabins, your choice boils down to personal priorities. If you're only using it to sleep, an interior room is fine. But if you're like me and enjoy quiet moments with a good book, a balcony cabin is worth the splurge. There's something soothing about watching the ocean stretch into infinity, knowing the world is just a step outside your door.

## Packing for Tropics and Tundra

Packing for a cruise that spans sunny beaches, and icy Antarctica is no small feat. For the tropics, think light, breezy clothes, sandals, sunscreen and a wide-brimmed hat. Nobody wants to match the lobster buffet.

For Antarctica, layers are your lifeline. A warm, insulated jacket, windproof outerwear, waterproof boots, gloves and a hat will keep you cozy while you marvel at penguins. And yes, sunscreen is a must. Snow glare burns are no joke.

Don't forget a light jacket for breezy evenings on deck, comfortable shoes for excursions and that book you've been "meaning to read" — perfect for pretending to relax while you people-watch. Adventure, after all, is about being prepared and looking the part.

FINAL THOUGHTS: **Embrace the Journey**

Cruising as a solo traveler is what you make of it. It's a unique blend of independence and connection, luxury and simplicity. Whether you're sipping a cocktail on the top deck, exploring a bustling port or savoring a quiet moment with the sea as your companion, the experience is yours to shape. So, pack your bags, set your expectations and get ready for a voyage that's as memorable as you are. Bon Voyage!

# TRAINS, TAXIS AND OTHER FORMS OF TRANSPORTATION

Tour Bus, Cienfuegos, Cuba

"Travel is about the gorgeous feeling of teetering in the unknown." Anthony Bourdain

# CHAPTER 11

**Traveling by Train: A Love Story (Mostly)**
Europe's trains are, in a word, fabulous. Smooth, fast, clean and affordable — what more could you want? Oh, and did I mention the food is decent? You're not getting a five-course meal, but you won't starve. However, I must burst the bubble for you romantics out there: You might not see as much scenery as you'd like. Those dreamy, postcard-perfect vistas are often blocked by shrubbery that seems specifically planted to ruin your Instagram dreams. Sometimes it feels like the shrubbery's main purpose is to mock you as you speed by, oblivious to the beauty just out of sight.

Let's talk **Euro Rail Passes**. These shiny little tickets can only be purchased before you leave the U.S., so don't get too comfortable thinking you'll snag one mid-Europe. They're great...until they're not. Hidden costs, like mandatory reservations on certain routes, can sneak up on you faster than you can say *bonjour*. Trust me, I learned this the hard way on a Basel-to-Berlin trip. Picture me, nonchalant with my pass, suddenly locked in a two-hour saga at the ticket counter, battling language barriers. (My non-existent French and German didn't help.) By the time it was resolved, I felt like I'd earned a diploma in miscommunication. Lesson learned: Know the rules and make those pesky reservations in advance.

Also, avoid student travel seasons unless you enjoy playing musical chairs: train edition. Spring for a first-class ticket — it's worth it to have a guaranteed seat and avoid sitting on your suitcase in the hallway while eyeing someone else's seat with envy. First-class also means fewer crowds, which is a blessing when you're trying to enjoy your snack in peace without elbowing your neighbor.

On later trips, I skipped the pass and bought tickets as needed. Turns out this can be more flexible and cheaper depending on your plans. For instance, an Italian train from Rome to Florence and then Milan? Cheaper, faster, and infinitely less hassle than flying. No two-hour airport security lines or endless baggage claims. Just hop on the train and go. Italy, you win this round.

### The Solo Traveler's Train Dilemmas

Solo train travel has its quirks. First, your luggage is your clingy travel buddy — don't even think about leaving it alone while you use the restroom. Befriending a family nearby to watch your stuff is a smart move, though I wouldn't trust strangers with my bags *and* my snacks. Priorities, people!

As for sleeping on trains, let's just say it's not my style. Call me paranoid, but I like my doors secure and my wits about me. The thought of dozing off while my suitcase slowly rolls into the arms of a thief is enough to keep me wide awake. You do you, though. Maybe you'll find a sleeper cabin that feels safe and cozy.

And if you're a senior, don't forget to milk those discounts. In France, for a modest fee you can obtain a Senior Pass saving you a bundle on fares. Even with the pass purchase, my train ticket cost less than flying — and I didn't have to deal with grumpy TSA agents.

### The Train Survival Guide

Here are a few essentials for train newbies (and forgetful veterans):

- Know your **class, coach, and seat number**. Wandering aimlessly looking for Wagon 7 is not fun.
- Double-check the **track/platform number**. European trains leave promptly. They're not like that one friend who's always 15 minutes late.
- Keep an eye out for overhead signs showing where each coach will stop. Nothing says "rookie" like sprinting down the platform with your suitcase in tow.
- Don't assume railway staff speak English. In Russia, I once tried to decipher directions through hand gestures that felt more like a game of charades. Spoiler: I lost.

### Taxis: A Love-Hate Relationship

For every city I've visited, there's a taxi story. Some are

downright terrifying, others are laugh-out-loud funny, and a few make you question the very fabric of humanity. Taxis, it seems, are where the true adventure begins — because there is nothing quite like haggling over a fare, clinging to your seatbelt (if there is one) or trying to decode a driver's unique interpretation of local geography.

Official taxis are your safest bet. Stick to taxi lines or have your hotel call one. Never, *ever* accept rides from random strangers offering you a "good deal." That's not a deal; it's a cautionary tale waiting to happen.

In Buenos Aires, for example, legit taxis are marked "Radio Taxi." But one hot, desperate afternoon, I ignored all common sense and climbed into an unmarked cab. Big mistake. Halfway to my destination (or maybe nowhere near it), I jumped out and made my escape. Pro tip: Give an intersection, not your actual hotel address, to avoid unwanted reunions.

And the change scam? It's real. If your fare is 12 pesos and you hand over 20 pesos, expect to see zero change. Just hand the driver exact fare or prepare to contribute to their unofficial retirement fund.

If you're bold, try this trick: Fake a loud phone call to a local friend complaining about how the last driver overcharged you. Both times I've tried this; the driver suddenly became much more reasonable. Coincidence? I think not.

Guidebooks love to remind you to make sure the taxi meter is turned on. Great advice in theory, but let's be honest — it doesn't stop a creative driver from taking the scenic route (also known as the "tourist detour") to pad the fare. Since you don't know the city, you probably won't realize what's happened until you're Googling the shortest route later that night, muttering to yourself.

To avoid surprises, always ask how much the ride will cost before even opening the taxi door. Don't be shy about negotiating a set price, either. Sure, it might feel awkward, but it's better than arriving at your destination feeling like you've just funded the driver's vacation.

Nighttime brings a new twist: the dreaded "night rate". Returning to Rome from Naples on the last train one evening, I discovered the fare from the station to my hotel was double what I'd paid that morning. When I (politely) asked the driver why, he gave me a surly shrug and said, "Lady, do you want to go to your hotel or not?" Let's just say my bargaining skills weren't up to the challenge that night.

But here's a fun curveball: If your destination is *too close*, taxis might outright refuse to take you, leaving you to fend for yourself. After a late-night performance at Cemil Topuzlu in Istanbul, I learned this the hard way. No one wanted to bother with my short ride to the hotel. I ended up speed-walking through quiet streets at midnight, wondering why common sense — like taking a quick fare and immediately returning for another — wasn't part of their business model. Too logical?

Pro tip: Always carry your hotel's card with you. It's your lifeline when taxi drivers suddenly don't "understand" the address, pretend they don't know the place (like in St. Petersburg), or pass you off to another driver for reasons known only to them. Having the card can save you from frustration — or a midnight workout — when you're just trying to get back to your room in one piece.

Public Transportation: **A Global Treasure**

Everywhere outside the U.S. seems to have mastered

public transport. Trains, trams, buses, ferries — they're all efficient and affordable. Some are even free for seniors (looking at you, Prague). Others, like Paris, are easy to navigate but come with a thigh-burning number of stairs. Honestly, by the end of my Parisian subway adventures, I had calves Michelangelo could've sculpted.

The best part? Public transportation keeps you grounded (literally) and immersed in local culture. Plus, it's often cheaper and more reliable than hailing a cab — especially late at night.

### Ride Shares

Uber and Lyft have revolutionized travel, though they come with quirks. Not all countries have them, and in some places, they're named differently or operate under strict rules. Always ask your hotel or host about local ride-share apps.

In Milan, I booked a private driver through the hotel concierge when taxis went on strike. Bonus: it was cheaper than a taxi and the car didn't smell like desperation and old fries. Ride shares are usually a win, but finding the pickup spot in an unfamiliar city? It's like trying to decode hieroglyphics without a Rosetta Stone. Coordinates would help if you had a compass and knew how to use it.

### Renting Cars: Proceed with Caution

I'm not brave enough to rent a car solo in a foreign country unless they drive on the right side of the road *and* speak English. Renting is affordable, but gas prices will make your wallet cry. If you're over 70, double-check age restrictions — some companies might turn you away.

One memorable trip involved me navigating while a friend drove through the French countryside in a stick shift. It was fun, scenic, and surprisingly stress-free — until we hit a roundabout. Then it was every woman for herself.

### The Bottom Line

Traveling solo comes with challenges, but it's all part of the adventure. Whether you're speeding through Europe on a train, haggling with a taxi driver, or navigating public transport, the key is preparation — and a sense of humor. So, pack your bags, plan and get ready for the stories you'll laugh about later.

# TOURS

Tour Guide, Machu Picchu, Peru

"I've not ceased being fearful; I've gone ahead despite the pounding in my heart that says: turn back, turn back, if you go too far."
Erica Jong

## CHAPTER 12

*𝒜*dventures in Touring: Lessons from a Reluctant Tourist

It all started with a friend's irresistible pitch: "Eighteen days in Thailand! Tigers! Adventure"! As a devoted cat lover — big, small, or digital meme — this sounded like a dream. Tigers and adventure? Sign me up. Little did I know, this was my first step into the world of *organized group tours*, a realm that, for better or worse, would teach me valuable lessons about my travel preferences. Spoiler: It wasn't exactly the feline fantasy I'd imagined.

### The Allure (and Annoyance) of Package Tours

Here's how these tours work: A guide magically orchestrates your itinerary, transportation and luggage logistics. Your breakfasts and hotels? Pre-arranged. Your tips, souvenirs and airfare? That's on you. You get whisked from one "must-see" attraction to the next, encouraged to shop ("support the economy!") and occasionally introduced to locals — always pre-vetted and suspiciously eager to sell you something.

While this setup is great for anyone craving a stress-free adventure, it became clear that rigid schedules and I don't mix. Sure, I loved riding river rafts and checking off cultural landmarks, but I missed the freedom to wander, linger or strike up conversations with intriguing strangers.

### THE TURNING POINT

Picture this: On a cold rainy day in Bangkok, the bustling streets are alive with energy. After an obligatory stop at the Jim Thompson shop (because *every* tour *must* include a shopping detour), I stopped to take off my cold, wet socks. Glamorous, right? A young man on a motorcycle caught my attention. We struck up a conversation about the area's unique architecture and for a moment I felt like a true traveler.

Then I looked up.

My group had vanished.

Cue a mad sprint, weaving through Bangkok's chaos, only to arrive at the train station just in time to see my group disappearing behind the closing doors of the elevated train. In that moment, I knew group tours weren't for me. Cutting short genuine experiences to stay on schedule? No, thank you. From that day on, I swore to travel on my own terms — or at least in smaller, more flexible groups.

### WHY TOURS **and I Just Don't Get Along**

To be fair, group tours have their perks. Someone else manages logistics so you can focus on sightseeing without worrying about transportation or hauling luggage. But for me, the trade-offs — early mornings, rushed visits and obligatory shopping stops — weren't worth it.

Let's not forget the awkwardness of touring someone's private home alongside 15 other camera-wielding strangers. Or the relentless reminders to "support local businesses" by buying things you don't need.

The pace was always off too. Either we rushed through highlights so fast they blurred together, or we lingered far too long at places I could've skipped. And those crack-of-dawn departures? My inner night owl was not amused.

### The Rare Exceptions

That said, I haven't sworn off tours. Day trips? Those are doable. When my cruise docked in Granada, Spain, I joined a short excursion to the Alhambra. The itinerary was focused, the pace manageable and it had just enough structure to feel relaxed without sacrificing my independence.

I'm also a fan of hop-on, hop-off buses. They're perfect for getting the lay of the land in a new city and with a two-day ticket, they double as a transportation pass.

### The Giverny Debacle

Not all tours go smoothly, though. Take my ill-fated visit to Monet's Garden in Giverny. What was supposed to be a serene half-day escape turned into an endurance test. First, our assistant guide went AWOL, delaying our departure by an hour. Then, despite promises of "extra time" to make up for it, we were rushed through the gardens like contestants on a reality show.

When I strolled back to the parking lot, still mesmerized by Monet's lilies, I watched in horror as our bus *drove away*. My options? Panic? Or Problem-solve?

Spotting a nearby bus stop, I cobbled together an alternate route involving a local bus and a train from Vernon to Paris. Of course, I missed the first train and spent hours waiting for the next. By the time I hobbled back to my Paris hotel — pre-knee surgery, no less — I was ready to declare war on that tour company.

My complaints to their customer service department were met with polite indifference and an insistence that my confirmation number didn't exist. Lesson learned: Even reputable companies have their off days.

### Why I Prefer Solo Travel

If you enjoy having someone else handle the nitty-gritty details — lugging bags, arranging meals, planning routes — tours might be for you. But for me, travel is about freedom: The freedom to linger in a moment, speed through less interesting spots, sleep in or follow a whim down an unexpected alley.

### Tips for Surviving a Day Bus Trip

Should you find yourself on a day tour, a little preparation can make all the difference.

- **Water**: Hydration is key.
- **Layers**: Buses are either Arctic or tropical — never in between.

- **Camera or Phone**: It's the 21st century; no judgment if your "camera" makes calls too.
- **Comfortable Shoes**: Blisters are no one's friend.
- **Sunscreen & Hat**: Sunburns don't make great souvenirs.
- **Snacks**: Because hunger waits for no one.

And most importantly, pack a sense of humor. When things inevitably go sideways—because they can—it's better to laugh than cry.

### Final Thoughts

Traveling solo or in small groups may come with more responsibility, but for me, it's worth it. There's a joy in discovering the world on your own terms, guided by curiosity rather than a rigid schedule. So yes, I've not ceased being fearful — but I've learned to keep going, despite the pounding in my heart that says, *turn back.* After all, adventure is waiting — and it rarely happens on schedule.

# SPAS

Whirlpool, Hotel Ixtapan de la Sal, Mexico

"Massage is the only form of physical pleasure to which nature forgot to attach consequences." Robert Breault

## CHAPTER 13

For centuries, humanity has turned to spas for healing and rejuvenation, dating back to the ancient Greeks and Romans who knew the power of "taking the waters." Of course, they didn't have Instagram to document their relaxing retreats, but they had the right idea — mineral waters could soothe the body, refresh the spirit and probably make you forget about the toga that doesn't fit you quite right anymore.

Fast forward a few millennia and the modern spa experience has blossomed into an art form, where indulgence meets self-care. These days, going to a spa might seem like a frivolous luxury, but I've learned firsthand that it's one of the most worthwhile investments you can make for your health. And yes, there's a delicious irony in paying good money to spend a week doing "nothing" but relaxing, sweating, eating calorie-counted meals and wearing a robe everywhere like a character in a hotel commercial. But trust me — it's transformative. Especially if you're traveling solo.

. . .

### Why I Love **Solo Spa Trips**

Let me start with a confession: I adore solo spa trips. Not because I'm asocial (well, not *entirely*), but because there's something liberating about having no one to answer to. No debates about whether to try the deep tissue massage or the herbal wrap. No guilt about spending an entire afternoon napping by the pool. And, perhaps most importantly, no one to witness me enthusiastically demolishing a plate of gluten-free carrot cake that I told myself was a "vegetable."

Spas are perfect for the solo traveler because the environment is so welcoming. Whether it's over a shared meal or while lounging between treatments, you'll end up chatting with other guests. And if you're feeling less social, no one will bother you. It's your time, and the only schedule you must follow is the one filled with massages, yoga classes and a possible afternoon aquatics session that you'll talk yourself out of in favor of the steam room.

### First-timer Nerves: **Don't Sweat it Unless You're in the Sauna**

Let's talk spa etiquette because, let's face it, navigating your first spa experience can feel a bit like walking into an exclusive club where everyone but you know the rules, especially if you're in a foreign country.

On my first visit to a spa, I was clueless. What's the dress code? (Answer: robes for everything except breakfast and dinner.) Am I supposed to tip my massage therapist? (Yes, unless it's an all-inclusive spa where gratuity is part of the package.) Nothing disrupts a tranquil environment like the sound of a ringtone or a loud conversation. Keep your voice soft and soothing. A good rule of thumb is to channel your "bedroom voice."

If you feel like embracing your inner goddess and going completely bare, go for it. I've also learned that what you wear during treatments — or don't wear — is entirely up to you. At first, I was self-conscious and opted for modesty, but by day three, I was practically auditioning for an *au naturel* lifestyle. Spa etiquette can feel intimidating at first, but everyone else is just as clueless during their first visit. Relax — you're in good company.

### The Magic of Hot Stone Massages (and other Treatments)

Over the years, I've experimented with a variety of treatments, and a few have become my absolute favorites. Hot stone massages are at the top of the list. There's something magical about the sensation of warm, smooth stones melting away tension in your muscles. The moment the therapist places a heated stone in my hand, I'm transported to a state of relaxation so profound I'd swear my muscles forgot how to tense up.

Another standout for me is the aromatic massage. The combination of soothing touch and calming essential oils feels like a hug for the soul.

There's also an endless menu of other treatments: facials that make you glow like you've just come back from vacation (which you may have), body scrubs that leave your skin feeling softer than a baby and wraps that make you look like a human burrito. It's indulgent, yes, but it's also deeply restorative. And don't even get me started on the joy of soaking in a mineral pool while contemplating how you've somehow managed to schedule relaxation as a daily task.

And then there are the quirky treatments I've stumbled upon during my travels. Have you ever heard of Ichthyotherapy? It's better known as a fish pedicure. In places like Bali, Thailand and Mexico, tiny Garra rufa fish nibble away at the dead skin on your feet. The sensation is...well, ticklish, to say the least. One time, after realizing the fish weren't interested in my feet, I switched tanks, only to remember that I'd had a fresh pedicure earlier that day. Pro tip: skip the salon if you're planning a fish spa session.

I've also discovered that spa treatments can come to the rescue in unexpected ways. After an exhausting day exploring San Francisco's famously steep streets, I treated myself to a leg massage that revived me just in time for an evening at the opera. It's amazing how the right treatment can turn a "meh" day into a magical one.

## A Balancing of Socializing and Solitude

One of my favorite parts of spa life is the mix of social opportunities and blissful solitude. Breakfasts and lunches are especially easy times to meet other guests, usually over shared experiences like an intense yoga class or the shared joy of discovering the dessert menu isn't calorie-free and that carrot cake does not count as a vegetable.

Some of my favorite conversations have happened in the lounge areas between treatments. Whether we're trading book recommendations, sharing tips about the best facials or commiserating over how sore we are from an overzealous hike, there's a camaraderie among spa-goers that's hard to replicate elsewhere. Of course, if you'd rather keep to yourself, you can always retreat to a quiet corner with a good book or, let's be honest, a very long nap.

### It's Not Just Pampering: It's Health Maintenance

A week at a spa isn't just about massages and mineral soaks. Many spas offer fitness classes, hiking trails, gyms, aquatic programs and more, making it as much about physical health as mental rejuvenation. I've tried everything from water aerobics (fun) to yoga to guided nature walks where I learned that yes, my calves *can* cramp if the incline is steep enough.

The meals are another highlight. Spa cuisine is designed to be healthy, but it's also shockingly delicious. I'm still dreaming about the almond-crusted salmon I had last year — who knew healthy food could feel like an indulgence?

### More Than Just Pampering: Why Spas Matter

At first glance, a spa day might seem like a splurge, but the benefits run far deeper than surface-level indulgence. Spas provide a rare opportunity to pause, reflect and truly care for yourself in a way that's often neglected in our busy lives. Whether it's the healing power of touch, the calming effects of a hot soak, or simply the act of slowing down, spas remind us that wellness isn't a luxury, it's a necessity.

So, if life ever feels overwhelming, consider escaping to a spa. Slip into that robe, embrace the rituals and let yourself be cared for. You might just find that the most valuable thing you take home isn't a souvenir but a renewed sense of calm and clarity.

### Final Thoughts: Spa Life for the Win

If you've never treated yourself to a solo spa trip, I can't recommend it enough. It's a chance to recharge, recenter and return to the world feeling like the best version of yourself. Plus, where else can you lounge in a robe, eat gourmet food and have your muscles turned to jelly — all while technically doing something productive for your health?

So go ahead, book that spa getaway. Slip into that robe, embrace the rituals and let yourself be cared for. You just might find that the most valuable thing you take home isn't a souvenir but new friends and some book recommendations.

# ECOTOURISM

Dunn River Falls, Jamaica

*"Take Only Memories, Leave Only Footprints" (misattributed to Chief Seattle, 1854; actually, penned by Ted Perry, 1972, for the film "Home")*

# CHAPTER 14

The phrase "Take only photographs and leave only footprints" has become a travel mantra for the environmentally conscious. But here's the twist: It's often attributed to Native American wisdom, even though some native cultures believe photographs can steal your soul. Regardless of who first said it, the sentiment is timeless.

Think about it. What would happen if every tourist took a pebble as a keepsake from a beloved beach? In time, that beach would look more like a parking lot. Imagine Devils Tower in Wyoming or Uluru in Australia? Two stunning natural wonders eroded by visitors carrying away buckets of dirt as souvenirs. Before long, there'd be nothing left to marvel at except a plaque reading, "Once a Majestic Wonder, Now a Hole." The message here? Snap a photo, savor the moment, but leave nature intact for the next wanderer.

### Ecotourism: Travel with Purpose

While the term "ecotourism" might sound trendy, the

concept has been around for centuries. Scientists were original ecotourists, combining exploration with research. Whether they were collecting rare specimens, counting wildlife populations or excavating ancient ruins, these researchers often invited regular folks to join the adventure. For the scientists, it meant extra hands to help with the heavy lifting. Locals benefitted from money spent by the visitors. For the volunteers, it was an extraordinary opportunity to learn about nature, science, and the local culture while dodging swarms of mosquitoes and wrestling with tents. Some even went on to pursue careers in science, proving that a little mud and curiosity can go a long way.

In modern times, Costa Rica has emerged as a poster child for ecotourism. With its lush rainforests, rich biodiversity and commitment to sustainable tourism, it's the go-to destination for travelers looking to connect with nature. Jamaica has taken a different approach with its concept of "community tourism." Here, the focus is on the locals. Residents provide accommodations, run tours, curate activities, ensuring that the money spent by tourists stays within the community. It's tourism with heart and a healthy dose of practicality.

But don't confuse ecotourism with the usual whirlwind checklist of tourist hotspots. It's not about snapping a quick selfie at the Top 10 Instagram-worthy spots before rushing to the next location. It's about slowing down, soaking in the experience, and maybe even learning something new. Yes, learning on vacation — it's not as scary as it sounds.

## The Carbon Footprint Dilemma

Every so often, an article pops up asking if we should all

give up flying to save the planet. While the idea of traveling the world without ever boarding a plane is noble, it's not always practical. What's more realistic is making thoughtful choices about how we travel.

Carbon offset programs have become popular for eco-conscious travelers. Many promise to plant trees to balance out your flight's emissions. It's a lovely idea, but it does raise some questions: How many trees are planted? Do they thrive long enough to make a real impact? Are the companies behind these initiatives as transparent as they claim? The answers aren't always clear.

But you don't need to rely on offset programs to reduce your carbon footprint. Small, everyday decisions can make a big difference. Walk more — your feet are free, eco-friendly and they'll thank you later (once you get past the blisters). Opt for public transportation whenever possible. Buses, subways and trains often produce less pollution per passenger than cars. Bonus points if the vehicles are electric or powered by biofuels.

Of course, sustainability isn't just about transportation. It's about consuming thoughtfully, supporting local businesses and respecting the environments you visit. It's about finding a balance between satisfying your wanderlust and preserving the beauty of the planet for future generations.

### A Word on Opinions

One of the trickiest parts of eco-friendly travel is figuring out where to draw the line. Should you always choose the greenest option, even if it costs more or takes twice as long? Should you avoid flying altogether or just reduce the number of your flights? There's no one-size-fits-all answer. Each traveler must weigh their priorities and make decisions that align with their values.

What doesn't help? Judgment from others. No one wants to be lectured about their choice to fly across the Atlantic instead of taking a weeks-long boat ride. Encouraging responsible travel is great; shaming people for their choices is not. After all, the goal is to inspire change, not spark arguments.

**THE FINAL WORD: Tread Lightly, Travel Thoughtfully**

At its core, ecotourism is about more than reducing your impact. It's about creating positive change. It's about connecting with the natural world, learning from the communities you visit and leaving each place a little better than you found it.

So, take the photos, leave the footprints and skip the bucket of dirt. And remember, the most important souvenir you can bring home is a story worth sharing — preferably one that doesn't involve you accidentally toppling a rock formation in a protected park. Or a Santeria shrine.

# PHYSICAL AND MENTAL HEALTH

Exercising on the Seine, Paris, France

*"The groundwork for all happiness is good health".* Leigh Hunt

*"Your body hears everything your mind says"...* Thales

# CHAPTER 15

## The Real Travel Essentials

Confined to a hospital bed for nine excruciating days, battling sepsis and teetering on the edge of survival, I was jolted into a harsh reality: My body wasn't the fortress I'd believed it to be. Weak, wobbly and incapable of walking a straight line — without a sip of alcohol to blame — I realized I needed to rebuild from the ground up. (Imagine failing a sobriety test while sober. That would've been a story for the ages.) If I was serious about continuing my solo adventures, I had to get proactive.

That's when a personal trainer entered the scene, armed with exercises and an encouraging smile that bordered on sadistic. I learned to strengthen muscles I didn't know I had and worked on balance and coordination that had long been taken for granted. Fast forward a few months and I was standing taller, walking steadier and — most importantly — feeling like I could take on the world again. I haven't fallen and my confidence has blossomed like wildflowers after a rainstorm.

If you're planning to travel solo — or just want to avoid face-planting while reaching for a coffee mug — consider consulting a trainer or physiotherapist. They can tailor exercises to your needs, improving your balance, strength and overall sense of stability. It's never too late to start. And for my fellow adventurers, I've included a simple, illustrated routine in the appendices, perfect for cramped hotel rooms or your living room. Spoiler alert: It works wonders, but it may make you sweat.

**BOOSTING YOUR IMMUNE SYSTEM: Your Body's Travel Armor**

In my 50s I had a predictable, almost comedic travel pattern: enjoy the trip, start feeling run down, and — boom! Catch a cold just in time to spend my last days away sniffling and miserable. It didn't take a genius to figure out my immune system was waving the white flag after weeks of subpar sleep, airport germs and indulgent eating.

These days, I'm wiser, more cautious and equipped with strategies. At the first tickle in my throat or hint of fatigue, I double down on water, add an extra dose of vitamin C and prioritize sleep like a toddler after a tantrum. And guess what? It works. Sure, there's no perfect defense against illness, but being proactive has spared me plenty of misery.

Here's another golden tip: Build downtime into your itinerary. Tempting as it may be to cram your schedule with attractions, remember that vacations are supposed to be enjoyable — not marathons. On travel days, I make a point of not planning anything beyond reaching my destination. Sometimes, I'll stroll around the hotel to get my bearings, but that's about it. And let go of the fantasy that you can "see it all" in one trip. You can't. Trying will only leave you exhausted and longing for another vacation to recover from this one.

### Midday Pauses: Small but Mighty Recharges

One of the best habits I've cultivated while traveling is carving out time for intentional pauses. Whether it's lingering over a cappuccino at a bustling café, journaling on a park bench or people-watching in a charming square, these moments allow me to recharge and truly savor my surroundings.

When possible, I book accommodations close to the heart of the action. That way, if I hit a wall of fatigue I can retreat to my room for a quick power nap. It's a luxury, yes, but one that pays off in spades when it comes to maintaining energy and enthusiasm for the adventure.

### Altitude Sickness: A Sneaky, Unforgiving Foe

Altitude sickness is the underappreciated villain of travel. I used to think it only affected adventurers scaling Mount Everest or trekking through the Andes. How wrong I was. Growing up at 3,500 feet above sea level, I breezed through high-altitude escapades in my youth, driving up Pike's Peak without breaking a sweat. But now, living at sea level, even Albuquerque's modest 5,000 feet leaves me feeling like a deflated balloon.

And don't get me started on Tahoe. During a conference retreat there, I was hit so hard by altitude sickness that I oscillated between dry heaving and fantasizing about being teleported off the mountain. The moral of the story? Never underestimate the power of less oxygen.

If you're traveling to higher altitudes, give your body time to adjust. Spend a day or two at moderate elevations before climbing higher. Stay hydrated, skip the booze and be gentle with yourself. And if you're headed to Peru or a similar destination, embrace the local remedies, like cocoa tea. It's not just a cultural experience — it's a lifeline.

**MENTAL HEALTH: Navigating the Highs and Lows of Solo Travel**

Travel has a knack for magnifying our mental states. Planning a trip can spark joy and excitement, but crowded airports, lost luggage or unexpected delays can trigger stress and anxiety. Nothing steadies my nerves after a chaotic flight like seeing someone at baggage claim holding a sign with my name on it. There's something reassuring about knowing my transportation is sorted, even if they've misspelled my name (which happens more often than you'd think).

For many, travel can be a balm for grief or loss. It offers a change of scenery, a temporary escape and a chance to reconnect with oneself. Two weeks after my husband passed away, a dear friend invited me to Anguilla. We spent our days soaking up the sun, listening to the rhythm of the waves and finding solace in shared silences. It didn't erase the pain, but it gave me space to breathe and begin healing.

If anxiety or mood swings are part of your life, plan. Work with your therapist to create a mental health first-aid kit, complete with grounding techniques, calming exercises and anything else that helps you feel anchored. Don't forget to pack enough medication for the entire trip and maybe a little extra, just in case. Pro tip: Forgetting your meds in a foreign country is a logistical nightmare. Trust me on this one.

### SELF-CARE: The Key to Thriving on the Road

Self-care isn't a luxury — it's a necessity. From scheduling massages to practicing deep breathing, finding ways to nurture yourself while traveling pays dividends in energy, mood and overall enjoyment. Prioritize sleep, fuel your body with nutritious meals and hydrate like it's your job.

Small rituals, like journaling or meditating in the mornings, or evenings can also create a sense of stability, even when everything around you feels unfamiliar. Think of it as anchoring yourself amid the adventure.

### FINAL THOUGHTS: Invest in Yourself for Better Adventures

Physical and mental health are the unsung heroes of travel success. They're not as flashy as a well-curated Instagram post, but they're infinitely more valuable. Whether it's building strength, bolstering your immune system or tending to your mental well-being, these small investments in yourself will make every trip more enjoyable and fulfilling.

So, take care of yourself. Stretch before long flights, pause when you need to and laugh at the inevitable mishaps. Because at the end of the day, the best souvenirs aren't just the ones you bring home—they're the ones you carry within —resilience, joy and a sense of wonder.

# STAYCATION

B & B in Inverness, Scotland

"A journey of a thousand miles begins with a single step."
    Chinese proverb attributed to Lao Tzu

# CHAPTER 16

*E*mbracing Solo Travel Close to Home

Solo travel doesn't have to be a grand production involving faraway destinations, complicated itineraries or perfecting the art of packing your entire life into a carry-on bag. In fact, some of the most rewarding adventures can be found right in your own backyard — or at least close enough to get there and back in a day.

The magic of solo travel isn't about the miles you cover. It's about stepping outside your routine, seeing the world with fresh eyes and letting curiosity guide your way. It's a chance to be present, to wander without purpose and to connect with places and experiences that often go unnoticed in the hustle of everyday life.

### Why Explore What's Right Under Your Nose?

If you live in a city that is a tourist destination, it's easy to dismiss it as "just home." Why would you bother exploring the same landmarks and attractions that visitors flock to? The truth is, even locals overlook treasures in their own cities. When was the last time you walked the streets of your town with the same wonder and excitement as someone seeing it for the first time?

If your hometown isn't exactly a magnet for tourists, that's no reason to stay put. Adventure can be found anywhere: a neighboring town you've never visited, a stretch of scenic countryside just beyond city limits or even a hidden corner of your own neighborhood you've yet to explore. Sometimes, the best discoveries are the ones hiding in plain sight.

**THE FREEDOM of the Open Road**

When I lived in Atlanta, one of my favorite ways to recharge was to escape the city for a day. I'd hop in my car, turn up some music and head out with no real destination in mind. The goal wasn't to "get somewhere" but simply to enjoy the journey.

The landscape would shift as I left the urban sprawl behind, trading skyscrapers for open farmland and bustling streets for quiet country roads. Along the way, I'd stumble upon roadside fruit stands, mom-and-pop diners and tiny antique shops packed with curiosities.

The beauty of these trips was the freedom to take the scenic route, make impulsive stops and let the road lead wherever it wanted. There's something liberating about not having a set agenda — about embracing the unknown and discovering joy in the simplest of moments.

. . .

## Romanticizing the Solo Journey

On these drives, I often fancied myself as the protagonist in a novel. You know the type — someone seeking solitude and inspiration, escaping the chaos of the city for the peace of the countryside. There's something romantic about the act of solo travel, especially when you let yourself lean into the fantasy of it all.

Imagine a cup of coffee in a roadside café, the sunlight streaming through the window as you watch the world go by. Or a peaceful walk through a meadow, the only sound being the rustle of leaves and the occasional bird call. It's not Paris or Tuscany, but there's a certain magic in creating your own story, even in the most ordinary of settings.

## Turning the Mundane into an Adventure

Some of my most memorable adventures didn't even take me out of my city. Once, when my house was being fumigated for termites, I decided to treat the inconvenience as an opportunity. Instead of crashing on a friend's couch, I booked a room in a small boutique hotel in a neighborhood I'd always been curious about.

The area was a study in contrasts: sleek coffee shops next to boarded-up buildings, vibrant street art adorning crumbling walls and an energy that felt both chaotic and alive. With no home to retreat to, I spent days wandering through local parks, sampling food from hole-in-the-wall restaurants and soaking in the charm of a part of my city I'd never truly seen.

Even the less glamorous parts of the experience — the uncomfortable bed, the quirky plumbing in the hotel bathroom — became part of the story. It reminded me that travel doesn't have to be perfect to be memorable.

### The Desert in Bloom: A Lesson in Resilience

Another favorite solo escape has been day trips to the desert during wildflower season. Armed with my camera and a sense of wonder, I'd lose myself in the surreal beauty of the landscape.

There's something humbling about seeing delicate wildflowers thrive in an unforgiving environment. It's a reminder beauty often blooms in the most unexpected places.

### Simplicity Is the Secret to Adventure

The beauty of these close-to-home adventures is their simplicity. They don't require months of planning, elaborate budgets or complicated logistics. They're spontaneous, accessible and often just what you need to break free from the monotony of daily life.

Sometimes, it's the lack of expectations that makes these small escapes so magical. With no pressure to see or do everything, you're free to simply be present and let the experience unfold.

### Your Next Journey Might Be Just Down the Road

Whether it's a countryside drive, a weekend escape to a nearby town, or a staycation where you play tourist in your own city, solo travel doesn't have to mean crossing continents. It's less about distance and more about perspective.

No plane tickets or elaborate itineraries are required — just you, a bit of curiosity and a willingness to embrace the unexpected. Sometimes, the most rewarding journeys are the ones that start just down the road. And as for the best travel companion? You're already looking at them in the mirror.

# EPILOGUE

*Ready to go*

"Good girls go to heaven; bad girls go everywhere." Mae West

# THE GREAT SOLO EXPEDITION

## An Ode to Wandering Alone and Loving It

Solo travel. It's a phrase that conjures images of serene mountain peaks and sun-dappled cobblestone streets. Or maybe it's a perfectly framed Instagram shot of you, coffee cup in hand, gazing thoughtfully into the distance. But let's be real — solo travel is just as often about boarding the wrong bus, asking a stranger to take your picture and eating a questionable sandwich on a park bench because the menu was in a language you're certain was invented just to confuse tourists.

And yet, despite the occasional mishaps (or perhaps because of them), solo travel is one of life's most rewarding experiences. It's a journey not only across new landscapes but also into the depths of your own courage, adaptability and resourcefulness. It's about discovering that yes, you can handle being in a city where no one speaks your language — and you can thrive there, all while racking up stories you'll tell for years.

## Tiny Steps, Big Rewards

Let's start with the basics: You don't need to launch your solo travel career with a three-month trek through the Amazon or a one-way ticket to Mongolia. No, your first adventure can — and perhaps should — be something much more manageable. A weekend road trip. A train ride to the next state. Even just an overnight stay at a bed-&-breakfast where you don't know anyone except the proprietor and even, they only know your name because it's on the reservation.

Why start small? Because solo travel, like anything worth doing, is a skill you build over time. Think of it as a muscle — one that gets stronger with practice and just a pinch of trial and error.

The first time you try to navigate an unfamiliar public transportation system, it might feel like trying to decode ancient hieroglyphics while everyone around you seems to have a secret manual. The second time, it's more of a puzzle — challenging, but solvable. By the third or fourth solo trip, you're a seasoned pro, offering directions to bewildered tourists as if you've lived there your whole life. (Of course, you might still double-check Google Maps under the table, but they don't need to know that.)

The point is each experience builds on the last. Start small, take your time and before you know it, you'll be gliding through adventures like you were born for this — because really, you were.

## Embracing Mistakes

Here's a truth about solo travel that no glossy travel blog will tell you: You will mess up. You'll take the wrong train, mispronounce something important, or realize halfway through dinner that you ordered an appetizer meant for six people. But these moments? They're pure gold. They're the stories you'll treasure long after the trip is over. Like the time I ordered what I thought was a local delicacy in a quaint café, only to discover it was some sort of pickled organ meat. (Pro tip: Always ask before assuming "specialité du chef" is a good idea.) Or the time I got lost in Buenos Aires and ended up in the middle of a protest where I was mistaken for an activist and handed a sign. Or next to the snake charmer in Tangier.

Mistakes are the seasoning of solo travel. They turn ordinary trips into extraordinary adventures. And, more importantly, they remind you that perfection is overrated.

**Dining Alone: From Awkward to Awesome**

Ah, dining alone — the ultimate test of solo travel confidence. For many first-time solo travelers, the thought of sitting alone at a restaurant feels like the stuff of nightmares. What will people think? Will the waiter judge me? Should I bring a book to avoid looking lonely?

Let me assure you: Dining alone is one of life's great pleasures. You can order exactly what you want, linger as long as you like and revel in the freedom of not having to share your dessert. And the people-watching? It's unparalleled.

I once spent an entire meal in Helsinki imagining the life story of a couple seated near me. Were they spies? Secretly breaking up? Planning a heist? (Spoiler: They were probably just tourists like me, but it was fun to pretend.) Dining alone is a chance to savor not just the food but the atmosphere, the ambiance and the delightful realization that you can absolutely handle this — and enjoy it.

**The Art of Getting Lost**

Every solo traveler gets lost. It's practically a rite of passage. Maps fail, GPS glitches and sometimes you just wander too far because you're enchanted by the scenery.

But here's the thing: Getting lost is often the best part of the journey. It's how I discovered an incredible street market in Athens, where I ate figs so fresh they tasted like sunshine. It's how I stumbled upon a tiny art gallery in Buenos Aires, tucked behind an unassuming storefront, where the artist himself offered me a tour. And in Venice, where getting lost is practically a sport, it's how I found the perfect gelato shop — and, eventually, my way back to the main square.

Getting lost teaches you to trust yourself, to ask for help when you need it and to see detours not as setbacks but as opportunities.

**Life Lessons from the Road**

Solo travel isn't just about seeing new places — it's about seeing yourself in a new light. It's about discovering that you can navigate a foreign subway system, charm your way through a language barrier or fix a broken suitcase zipper with nothing but a paperclip and sheer determination.

It's also about embracing the unexpected kindness of strangers. Like the shopkeeper in Vienna who offered me a chair and a glass of water when I was frazzled. Or the taxi driver in Buenos Aires who insisted on practicing his English and ended up giving me an impromptu history lesson about his city. Moments of connection remind you that, no matter where you go, humanity has a way of shining through.

\* \* \*

## A Final Push

If you're on the fence about traveling solo, let me gently nudge you toward the departure gate. The world is waiting — not for the perfect traveler, but for *you*. The curious, slightly nervous, wonderfully adventurous *you*.

Start small or go big; it doesn't matter. What matters is that you go. You'll make mistakes, you'll laugh, you'll learn, and you'll come back with stories that will outshine any souvenir.

So, pack your bag (lightly), double-check your passport and take that first step. Because solo travel isn't just about where you go — it's about who you become along the way. And trust me: The person you'll meet on this journey is someone incredible.

# APPENDICES

## PRE-TRAVEL PREP

**The Art of Leaving Without Losing Your Mind**

Planning a three-week (or longer) adventure may sound like a dream come true, but let's not sugarcoat the reality: the pre-departure checklist is as long as a CVS receipt. Still, with a little preparation, you can leave your house (and life) in good order without spiraling into chaos. Below is my approach for a long trip

**1. Pets**

Arrange for the care of your pet. This could involve boarding your pet, arranging for someone to stay in your home and look after them, or having someone drop by during the day to provide love and care. My solution has been a Vet Tech that works at my local Vet Clinic. She comes in once a day to care for my cats and sends me a video of them playing which makes my heart sing.

**2. Quietly Notify Friends and Family**

Let your close friends and family know about your travel

APPENDICES

plans, but resist the urge to post, "Off to Australia for three weeks!" on Facebook or Instagram. It's one thing to share pictures once you're back, but announcing your absence from home to the world? Not the smartest move security-wise.

### 3. Share a Slimmed-Down Itinerary

I keep my loved ones informed with a concise itinerary emailed before I leave. This usually includes the dates I'll be away, my destinations, and sometimes flight and hotel details. This way, they know where I am if they need to reach me, but I'm not overwhelming them with every detail.

### 4. Handle Your Mail Situation

Mail doesn't take vacations, so it's up to you to stop it or redirect it. If you don't, you'll return to a mailbox overflowing with junk and important letters crammed into impossible angles. I often ask a neighbor clear out the junk mail from my home mailbox. I subscribe to a mailbox service, UPS. Pro tip: the folks at UPS appreciate being told when you won't be picking up your mail, so don't forget to notify them. Same applies to the US Postal service.

### 5. Alert Your Bank to Avoid Awkward Card Declines

Banks can get suspicious when your debit or credit card suddenly starts racking up charges in Berlin. Give them a heads-up about your travel dates and destinations, either by calling or using their online travel notification system. Some banks require you to fill out an online form, which is a lot less hassle than being stranded without access to funds because your card was flagged.

While you're at it, make digital copies of the front and

back of the cards you're bringing and save them to the Cloud or email them to yourself. This step saved my bacon once in South Africa, where a card mishap turned into a minor comedy of errors. Let's just say the phrase "travel learning curve" became relevant.

### 6. Enroll in the STEP Program

The State Department's Smart Traveler Enrollment Program (STEP) is free and a wealth of valuable information worth its weight in gold. It provides useful safety information for your destination. In case of a natural disaster, political unrest, or anything else that could disrupt your travel plans the government knows where you are. Enrolling takes just a few minutes and offers immense peace of mind.

### 7. Create a Detailed Itinerary for Yourself

I'm a big fan of detailed itineraries, not because I like to micromanage, but because they've saved me from countless headaches. Save one to the Cloud, carry a copy in your handbag, and stash another in your luggage. Include hotel addresses, confirmation numbers, and anything else you might need when Wi-Fi is scarce, and your phone battery is running on fumes.

### 8. Plan Airport Transportation

Getting to and from the airport can feel like an afterthought, but it's worth planning. For short trips, driving yourself and parking near the airport works fine. Some airport hotels even offer valet services where they'll store your car and bring it around when you return.

For longer trips, I prefer hiring an airport limo service. It's reliable, reasonably priced, and far less stressful than a shared shuttle service that doubles as an impromptu neighborhood tour. After one too many experiences of a no-show shuttle, I've sworn off them entirely. Ride-sharing apps like Uber and Lyft are also good alternatives although they can be more expensive than taxis

### 9. Charge All Your Devices Before You Leave

Don't count on airport outlets being available (or functional). Charge your phone, tablet, laptop, camera batteries, and anything else you plan to take. TSA wants electronics charged so they can see they are operational. While you're at it, pack a plug adapter compatible with your destination and a multi-outlet charger to avoid arguments over limited sockets. Apple users, rejoice: your charging cables already have built-in voltage converters, so no extra gadgets are needed. Add a portable battery pack to your list of necessary electronics.

### 10. Photograph Your Luggage (and Use Air Tags)

A quick snapshot of your luggage pre-trip could save you a lot of grief if it gets lost or damaged. Adding Air Tags or another tracking device can also give you peace of mind, especially when your bags seem to take their own detour during transit. If someone is collecting your luggage from the baggage claim area, this will expedite the process.

### 11. Empty the Fridge and Trash Bins

No one wants to return home to the fragrance of rotting produce or week-old garbage. Take a few minutes to clear out perishables from the fridge. Remove all trash from your home. If you're feeling generous, pass along any usable produce to a neighbor instead of letting it go to waste.

# APPENDICES

## 12. Pay Your Bills in Advance

Forgetting to pay bills while you're away can lead to unpleasant surprises when you return. Set up automatic payments for recurring expenses or knock them out before you leave

## 13. Pamper Yourself Pre-Flight

A good mani-pedi, haircut, or even a massage isn't just about vanity—it's about travel confidence. Looking your best can make long-haul flights and layovers feel less grueling. And if you're flying coach, where personal space is a myth, a pre-trip massage can be a sanity saver.

**Final Thoughts**

Traveling isn't just about the destination; it's also about ensuring your departure and return are as smooth as possible. With a little organization and a few extra steps, you can leave with peace of mind and come home to a house that hasn't turned into a scene from *Home Alone*. Bon voyage!

# PACKING

**A Skill Sharpened by Trial and Error**

Over the years, I've learned that no one-size-fits-all packing list will work for everyone. After many failed attempts to follow others' advice, I created my own list tailored to my quirks and needs. Packing, I've realized, is as much about who you are as where you're going.

**The Great Rolling Debate**

To roll or not to roll? It's the Hamlet of packing. Some travelers swear rolling saves space and prevents wrinkles. I've tried it, and honestly, the results didn't justify the hype. Wrinkles still appeared, and the extra space was negligible.

Then there was my ill-conceived experiment with vacuum-packing. The idea was brilliant in theory—compact, wrinkle-free clothing! But when I arrived at my destination, I realized I'd need scissors or a knife to open the bags, and I hadn't thought about where all those compressed items would go on the trip back. Lesson learned.

### Packing Cubes

What does work? Packing cubes. These little organizers have revolutionized the way I travel. They keep everything neat and make finding specific items so much easier. No more frantic, suitcase-exploding searches for that one elusive item.

For longer trips or when I'm checking luggage, I'll sometimes leave clothes on their hangers. That way, I can simply transfer them straight into a closet upon arrival. It's a small hack, but it saves time and effort.

### Weight and Dimensions: Know Before You Go

A luggage scale is a must. Overweight baggage fees can be outrageous, especially in certain countries. And don't forget to check your airline's size and weight restrictions. One airline's "carry-on approved" might be another's "too big for our bins." I've learned this the hard way—on one trip, my carry-on was fine for the first leg of my journey but had to be checked on the second because the bins were smaller.

Also, leave a little room in your luggage. Whether it's for souvenirs, unexpected finds, or just an extra bottle of wine, you'll appreciate the flexibility—or you'll end up buying another suitcase, which isn't the worst outcome either.

### Final Thoughts

Packing is a mix of art and science, with a healthy dose of trial and error. You'll forget something essential, overpack something useless, and almost certainly laugh about it later. In the end, what matters isn't what you bring but how you embrace the experience. Because let's face it—the best travel stories come from the unexpected moments, and no amount of planning can prepare you for those.

# SIGNALS THAT YOU MIGHT BE A U.S. TOURIST

**Appearance and Clothing:**

•**Baseball caps**: A quintessential American accessory, especially with sports logos.

•**Flashy or designer clothes**: Bold styles, expensive brands, or trend-heavy items.

•**Baggy sweat clothes and hoodies**: Emphasizes comfort over fashion, a U.S. staple.

•**North Face fleeces**: Popular with travelers for their practicality.

•**Logos on shirts**: Wearing visible brand names or slogans is common.

•**Fanny packs**: Practical but distinctly touristy.

•**Oversized backpacks**: Often packed for any and every occasion.

•**Flip-flops (in non-beach settings)**: Associated with casual, laid-back American culture.

\* \* \*

### Behavior at Restaurants:

•**Asking for WIFI as soon as you sit down**: Indicates connectivity is a high priority.

•**Raising your hand or snapping fingers for service**: A sign of impatience or unfamiliarity with local dining etiquette.

•**Asking for ice with drinks**: Americans' preference for ice-cold beverages stands out.

•**Expecting refills**: Bottomless cups are a U.S. custom, not universal.

•**Using knife and fork in "cut and switch" style**: The American habit of switching hands after cutting food is distinct from European styles.

### General Behavior:

•**Talking loudly**: Americans are often perceived as boisterous in public spaces.

•**Eating while walking**: A quick-meal-on-the-go culture isn't common everywhere.

•**On the phone or placing it face-up on the table**: A visible attachment to devices.

•**Carrying water bottles**: Prioritizing hydration wherever you go.

•**White teeth**: Reflects the American emphasis on dental care and cosmetic dentistry.

### Accessories Overload:

•**Wearing all the accessories**: Sunglasses, hats, watches, cameras, and more all at once.

This list, while playful, highlights cultural habits that might stand out abroad. Embracing these differences can make for great conversations with locals! Or maybe, you just want to blend in.

# RESOURCES

**Challenged individuals:**
  Society for Accessible Travel & Hospitality (SATH) wow! if use only one this is it
  TSA (can request for accommodations and special screening procedures)
  Wheelchair - contact the Airline or your travel agent to arrange
  Air Carrier Access Act (ACAA) provides legal protections for individuals with disabilities
  Disability Rights Education Defense Fund and Accessible Travel Solutions
  American Hearing a research agency with numerous educational articles
  Disability.org travel tips for persons with disabilities

**Vision-Impaired Travelers**
  APH Connect Center: A hub of tips and tools for navigating the world with low vision.
  American Council of the Blind: Advocacy and travel tips

# RESOURCES

for the visually impaired.

**Hearing impaired**
Ascetist travel tips for hearing impaired
Associated audiologist more travel tips for hearing impaired

# PLACES TO START YOUR SOLO ADVENTURES

## (BASED ON MY OWN TRIAL, ERROR, AND OCCASIONAL HILARITY)

Starting a solo journey can feel a bit daunting but fear not—I've made plenty of rookie mistakes, so you don't have to. Whether you're easing into the experience or ready to dive headfirst into the unknown, here's a list of destinations I've tested. Some were smooth sailing, and others… well, let's just say I've got stories.

**The United States: The Ultimate Staycation**

Why travel far when your own backyard is full of surprises? Book a hotel in your city, pretend you're from out of town, and explore like a tourist. The key here is no cheating. Forgot your phone charger? Too bad—hit the local pharmacy or the overpriced hotel gift shop. Feel the thrill of discovering what your hometown is like for someone who doesn't already know where the good pizza place is.

**English-Speaking Countries: Training Wheels for Solo Travel**

Start with countries where you won't need Google Translate every five minutes:

- **Great Britain**: Cozy pubs, castles, and accents that make everything sound polite—even when they're annoyed.
- **Ireland**: Warm people, lush landscapes, and enough Guinness to make you forget you're traveling alone.
- **Scotland**: Lochs, bagpipes, kilts, scotch, haggis, and impressive geographical diversity.
- **Canada**: Our polite northern neighbors offer dazzling scenery and a universal love of maple syrup.
- **Australia & New Zealand**: Beautiful beaches, breathtaking mountains, and plenty of "no worries" vibes.

**Countries Where English is a Second Language (But a Close Second)**

Once you're feeling bold, branch out to places where English isn't the primary language, but you'll still find plenty of help if needed:

- **Belgium**: Waffles, chocolate, frittes, mussels, and beer—need I say more? And don't forget the diamonds and lace
- **Germany & Austria**: Efficient trains, stunning architecture, and schnitzel that will make you swoon.
- **France**: Just learn to say Bonjour! and Merci, and

you're halfway to charming the locals. Bonus: Croissants!
- **Scandinavia**: These countries have some of the happiest people on Earth—and they all speak better English than you do.
- **Netherlands**: Amsterdam's canals are a solo traveler's dream. Just watch out for the bicycles—they will not stop for you.

**A Little More Adventurous: Testing Your Travel Mettle**
Ready to step out of your comfort zone? These destinations are safe, friendly, and offer plenty of wow-factor:

- **Greece**: Blue domes, whitewashed walls, and sunsets that will make your Instagram followers jealous.
- **Portugal & Spain**: Affordable, sunny, and brimming with history and tapas. What's not to love?
- **Hungary & Czech Republic**: Budapest and Prague are postcard-perfect—and way cheaper than Western Europe.
- **Croatia**: Think Game of Thrones scenery, minus the dragons. Plus, the Sea Organ.
- **Romania**: Visit Dracula's Castle and then laugh nervously when your power goes out that night.
- **Africa**: Yes, it's a big continent, but consider starting with a safari in South Africa, North Africa's bustling souks in Morocco or Pyramids of Egypt.

### Countries for the More Daring (Or Linguistically Gifted)

Here's where things get a bit tricky. If you're fluent in the local language—or have friends who are—it's worth considering. Otherwise, you might end up playing a game of charades with a taxi driver.

- **Russia**: Beautiful, complex, and sometimes a little baffling. Proceed with caution—and a Cyrillic phrasebook.
- **Southeast Asia & China**: Amazing food, rich history, and vibrant cultures, but navigating solo without some language skills can feel like a real-life escape room.

### Mexico, Central, and South America: A Cultural Balancing Act

Much of Latin America offers incredible solo travel opportunities, but it's not without its quirks. As a solo woman, you might find yourself treated like royalty... or misunderstood entirely. If you're older (like me), people tend to assume you're not "for hire," which is a relief. Still, be prepared for occasional cultural misinterpretations—and a lot of delicious food.

### Final Thoughts

Traveling solo is all about finding your stride, laughing at the occasional mishap, and discovering just how capable you are. Start where you're comfortable, push your boundaries bit by bit, and never forget to pack a sense of humor. Oh, and maybe a phone charger, just in case.

# EXERCISE DISCLAIMER

To reduce the risk of injury, before beginning this or any exercise program, please consult a healthcare provider for appropriate exercise prescription and safety precautions. The exercise instruction and advice presented are in no way intended as a substitute for medical consultation.

The following 6 exercises were developed without any gym equipment. Use common items found in your hotel room

**3-way Calf Stretch with towel x 5/5/5**
  Posterior Step with Over Head towel driver x 10/10
  Upper Trunk Rotation with towel x 10/10
  Marches in place (hold H2O bottle) x 20/20
  Anterior Step with Chest Press x 10/10
  Sit to Stand x 15

**3-way Calf Stretch 5/5/5**
  Roll up a small towel, place it on the floor, 1 to 2 feet from wall.

Place ball of rear foot on towel. You will stand on it. Hands on wall, each foot steps to left, center, and right 5 times each

**Posterior step with overhead towel driver 10/10**
    Roll up a towel as in the photo below
    Then stretch it as shown
    With each leg, step back and raise the towel.
    Make yourself tall by drawing in navel towards spine.
    Do this with each leg 10 times

## Upper Trunk Rotation with towel x 10/10
Hold the towel at chest level
Turn to the left and to the right as far as is comfortable
Try to keep the head looking straight ahead
Do this 10 times

## Marches in Place
Hold a water bottle in one hand
March 10 times on one leg.
Switch legs and march 10 more times

**Anterior Step with chest press 10/10**
    Start with stretched towel at chest height and near body
    Then step forward with one foot
    and force the towel away from you.
    With each leg, step forward 10 times
    as you force the towel forward

**Sit to Stand x 15**
    Stand with feet straight forward, keeping feet apart
    Sit 15 times. Hands can be at your side if desired.

EXERCISE DISCLAIMER

All photos in this set are by Marko Sanchez
    Marko Sanchez, CSCS
    Owner, Function Factory
    4490 W Point Loma Blvd
    San Diego, CA 92107

# MANAGING ANXIETY WHILE TRAVELING

**Tips for Coping with Stress on the Road**

Anxiety and depression are among the most common mental health challenges faced by individuals worldwide, and they often go hand in hand. Whether it's the general unease that accompanies life's uncertainties or the overwhelming panic of a full-blown anxiety attack, both conditions can impact one's quality of life.

Traveling, while exciting, can exacerbate these feelings, especially when faced with unfamiliar situations, travel mishaps, or stressors that arise while far from home.

Fortunately, there are several strategies and coping mechanisms available to help manage anxiety during travel, from therapeutic interventions to practical techniques that can provide immediate relief in moments of discomfort.

**A Spectrum of Experiences**

Anxiety can manifest in a wide range of ways, from mild worry and unease to more intense experiences such as panic attacks or generalized anxiety. It's important to recognize that the severity of anxiety can vary from person to person and from one situation to another. For some, anxiety may simply feel bothersome, like a nagging feeling of dread, while for others, it can be disabling, making it difficult to function or even leave the house.

The good news is that both anxiety and depression can be effectively managed with a combination of treatments. For many people, a combination of medication, such as SSRIs (selective serotonin reuptake inhibitors), and psychotherapy is a proven solution. If you are already on medication for anxiety or depression, it's crucial to ensure that your prescriptions are packed in your carry-on luggage when traveling. You never know when you might need to take them, especially in stressful or triggering situations, and you don't want to risk being without them.

**From Threat to Excitement**

One of the most effective tools for managing anxiety while traveling is reframing the anxiety experience. Often, the physical symptoms of anxiety—such as a racing heart, shallow breathing, and tightness in the chest—are similar to the physiological responses we experience when excited. By consciously reframing anxiety as a form of excitement, you can shift your perspective and make the experience feel more positive.

Instead of thinking of anxiety as a threat, try to reinterpret it as a sign that something exciting or new is on the horizon. This simple cognitive shift can help reduce the intensity of anxiety and create a more optimistic outlook on the situation.

*\*  \*  \**

## Techniques for Immediate Relief

When anxiety strikes, especially during travel, having a few simple techniques at your disposal can make a world of difference. One highly effective technique is the *3-3-3 rule*: Name three things you can see, three things you can hear, and three parts of your body. This grounding exercise helps refocus the mind and connect you to the present moment, which can interrupt the anxious thought patterns that often spiral out of control. It's a quick and easy tool to practice in airports, crowded tourist attractions, or even on a tour bus when you feel overwhelmed.

Deep breathing, meditation, yoga, and exercise are other excellent ways to calm the body and mind when anxiety strikes. Simple breathing exercises—like inhaling deeply for a count of four, holding for four, and exhaling for four—can help activate the body's relaxation response. For those who prefer movement, taking a walk, going for a run, or engaging in yoga can release built-up tension and reduce the physical symptoms of anxiety.

## Triggers While Traveling

Traveling, by nature, involves uncertainty and disruption to routine. These factors can trigger anxiety in many people, especially those with a predisposition to it. Anxiety tends to surface when we encounter situations that feel unsolvable or when things go wrong in unexpected ways.

For example, one might experience a surge of anxiety when plans go awry—like when a tour bus leaves you behind in a foreign city (I can claim personal experience here), and you have to figure out how to get home or back to your hotel alone. In these moments, the sense of being out of control can fuel the anxious thoughts, amplifying the experience.

In these high-stress situations, it's crucial to remember that anxiety often feeds on uncertainty. Focus on what you can control, such as taking a deep breath, remaining calm, and planning to resolve the issue. Remind yourself that you have the resources to handle the situation, and that problems are often solvable with time and a clear mind.

**Practical Strategies for Coping While Abroad**

Beyond immediate relaxation techniques, there are several other strategies that can help you manage anxiety during your travels. If you know that certain situations trigger your anxiety, take steps to minimize those triggers ahead of time. For example, if being in a crowded area or navigating public transportation causes anxiety, plan your route carefully or consider using a private transportation service.

Additionally, it's important to remember that you are not alone in these experiences. If you find yourself struggling, reaching out for emotional support can be incredibly helpful. Talk to a trusted friend or family member about your feelings or consider journaling to process your emotions. Sometimes, just articulating your worries can help diminish their power over you.

Another way to help manage anxiety is to focus on what reassures you. Think about the reasons you are traveling, the positive experiences you've had, and the goals you're working toward. Picture yourself reaching your destination or completing an activity you've been looking forward to. This mental visualization can help calm your mind and refocus your energy.

\* \* \*

**The Role of the Embassy**

For international travelers, it's also important to know where to turn in case of an emergency. If your anxiety becomes overwhelming, or if you find yourself in a situation where you need professional help, your country's embassy can be a valuable resource. They can provide you with information on local mental health services, and in some cases, assist with locating a healthcare provider.

# AFTERWORD

Managing anxiety while traveling is certainly a challenge, but it's not insurmountable. By using a combination of practical tools—such as breathing exercises, reframing anxiety as excitement, and practicing grounding techniques—you can reduce the impact of anxiety on your travel experience. Additionally, by focusing on what reassures you and seeking support when needed, you can create a more enjoyable and fulfilling journey. Remember, while anxiety is a common and often challenging condition, with the right tools and mindset, you can navigate it successfully and continue to enjoy the many benefits that travel has to offer.

**Managing Depression While Traveling: Strategies for Keeping Your Sanity**

Travel. The promise of adventure, self-discovery, and the joy of getting lost in a new city. But sometimes, that blissful fantasy gets interrupted by the not-so-glamorous travel companion: depression. Whether it's the stress of navigating new places, battling jet lag, or just the general chaos that

## AFTERWORD

comes with trying to catch a flight, depression can sneak up on you when you least expect it. And when you're miles away from your cozy couch and your favorite Netflix shows, managing those heavy feelings can feel like you're juggling flaming swords while riding a unicycle. But don't panic (or maybe do, just a little), because there are ways to navigate the emotional minefield of travel and keep your well-being in check.

**The Depression Dilemma: When Adventure Feels Like a Weight**

We've all been there—arriving in a new city, excited for the adventures ahead, only to feel a wave of sadness crash over you. You might experience low energy, negative thoughts, or that overwhelming sense of "I should be enjoying this, but I'm just... not." If it gets worse, it can feel like you're trudging through a fog, unable to shake off the sadness. Trust me, this isn't just you being dramatic (though, if you *are* being dramatic, I support that too). Travel's unpredictability, disrupted routines, and unfamiliarity with your surroundings can amplify those feelings, making it harder to shake off that mental cloud. But here's the good news: you *can* manage it.

**Step 1: Prioritize Sleep (Because Apparently, You Can't Function on Zero Hours of Rest)**

Let's talk sleep—because who knew that something so basic would be one of the hardest things to nail while traveling? Between jet lag, the thrill of new time zones, and those 3 a.m. flights you thought sounded like a good idea at the time, your sleep schedule can end up in total disarray. And let me tell you, a lack of sleep makes depression a lot more...

persistent. It's like giving your bad mood a VIP pass to your brain.

To combat this, treat sleep like it's your new best friend. Invest in a sleep mask (your eyes will thank you), earplugs, or noise-canceling headphones. If jet lag has you twisted, try adjusting to the local time zone gradually. Expose yourself to daylight (nature's caffeine) during the day and limit screen time at night. Your internal clock will slowly get the memo, and you'll feel less like a walking zombie.

**Step 2: Emotional Support: Don't Be a Lone Wolf**

Depression *loves* isolation. So, if you're traveling solo or feeling disconnected from loved ones, that loneliness can turn into a depressive breeding ground. But remember being away from home doesn't mean you're entirely alone. Pick up your phone and call someone you trust. Or if you're feeling more introspective, jot down your feelings in a journal. There's something cathartic about getting those swirling thoughts onto paper (even if it's just a complaint about the weird hotel pillow).

Also, try connecting with new people along the way. You'd be surprised at how engaging with a stranger, even if it's just asking for directions, can make you feel a little more grounded and a lot less lonely.

**Step 3: Immune Support: Don't Let Your Body Join the Meltdown**

When you're traveling, your immune system is basically like, "Hey, new germs! Let's get acquainted!" And guess what? Physical illness and depression go hand in hand. Feeling physically sick can make your mood tank even faster than your flight took off. So, hydrate like you're trying to revive a

## AFTERWORD

plant, eat a balanced diet (yes, those vegetables do exist in other countries), and take supplements to support your immune system. Wash your hands, use hand sanitizer, and do all those annoying yet essential things to keep germs at bay.

Taking care of your body isn't just about surviving travel—it's about thriving. When you feel physically well, your mental health tends to follow suit. So, treat your body like it's your travel companion, not your opponent.

**Step 4: Move It, Shake It: Don't Be a Couch Potato**

Exercise isn't just for getting your "beach body" (who are we kidding, the beach doesn't care). Movement, even in small doses, releases those magical mood-boosting endorphins. While it might be tempting to stay in bed and scroll through Instagram for hours (we've all been there), taking a daily walk, doing yoga, or hiking can do wonders for your mental state.

Pack comfy shoes and make walking part of your routine, whether you're wandering around a museum, strolling through a park, or exploring the hidden corners of a new city. If you're stuck in a hotel, check if they have a gym or sign up for a local yoga class. Even a few stretches can help release tension and put a little pep in your step.

**Step 5: Understand Your Triggers: Travel Can Be Both Stress and Relief**

Here's the kicker: travel can either be a catalyst for depression *or* a way to break free from the daily grind. For some people, leaving behind the stressors of home provides a much-needed mental reset. For others, the uncertainty, fast pace, and unfamiliarity can trigger feelings of overwhelm and anxiety. It's all about knowing your triggers and adjusting accordingly.

If travel is making you anxious, give yourself permission to slow down. Not everything has to be a whirlwind of sightseeing. Maybe it's okay to skip that tour and just enjoy a quiet coffee in a local café. You do you. Remember, it's not a race.

**Step 6: Small Steps for Big Relief**

Managing depression while traveling doesn't mean overhauling your entire existence. Sometimes, it's about the little things. Watch your favorite movie to lift your mood, or explore something new—a local play, a hobby you love, or even a cute pet café (hello, mood boost from cats). Avoid alcohol, because it's like giving your depression a megaphone, and instead, treat your body well with good food and self-care. Don't forget your lavender essential oil and chamomile tea for a dose of calm, and when all else fails, indulge in some dark chocolate—because science.

**Step 7: The 3 Cs: Catch It, Check It, Change It**

Now for a simple but powerful tool to manage those depressive thoughts: the 3 Cs. Catch it, check it, Change it. First, catch yourself when you start spiraling. Recognize those negative thoughts creeping in. Next, check whether those thoughts are based on reality or if you're just making mountains out of molehills. Finally, change the narrative. Reframe that thought into something positive or take small action to make yourself feel better.

* * *

AFTERWORD

**Step 8: Professional Help: Know When to Call in Reinforcements**

Sometimes, depression isn't something you can handle on your own. If things get too heavy, don't hesitate to reach out for professional help. Check if your travel insurance covers mental health services or contact your country's embassy for support. Knowing that you've got backup can be a game-changer.

**Conclusion: Travel Doesn't Have to Be a Battle**

Traveling with depression isn't easy, but with the right mindset and strategies, it's manageable. Prioritize sleep, stay connected with others, take care of your body, and keep moving. Recognize your triggers, practice self-care, and don't let the weight of depression steal your joy. With the right tools, you can turn your trip into a journey of growth, healing, and maybe even a few new favorite memories (and some great photos to show for it).

# SAMPLE ITINERARY

To create a reduced itinerary to leave with family and friends, eliminate some details such as reservation and confirm numbers. They don't need detailed info such addresses and times. It is your decision how much info you wish to share with family and friends.

| DATE | ACTIVITY | LOCATION | TIME |
|---|---|---|---|
| SEPT 5 | DL #484 | SAN-JFK, SEAT 3A | 0635 -1539 |
| 5-6 | DL #78 | JFK-PRG, Seat 2A | 1935-1000 |
| 6 | Car Service | Confirm # | |
| | Aria Hotel | Trziste 9  +420 225 334 111 reservation # | |
| | Jazz Cruise with food | Na Frantisku, molo 18 Stare Mesto Gate 18 confirm # | 2010 |
| 7 | Traditional Czech cooking | Thamova 32 +420 603 472 541 Metro Station Krizikova confirm # | 1430 |
| | Carmen (opera) | National Theatre | 1900 |
| 8 | Strahov Library | Strahovské nádvoří 1/132, 118 +420 233 107 718 (print out email) | 1230 |
| | Much Ado | Estate Theatre printout | 1900 |
| 9 | Kafka Museum | Clhelna 2b Mala Strana | 1100 |
| | Museum Communism | V Celnicihia 103/4 | |
| | Romeo & Juliet (ballet) | State Opera printout | 1900 |
| 10 | Free day to explore | W Square | |
| 11 | LOT #524 | PRG - WAW | 0955-1115 |
| | LOT# 3905 | WAW - KRK | 1325 - 1420 |
| | Car Service to hotel | Confirm # | |

SAMPLE ITINERARY

| Date | Activity | Location/Details | Time |
|---|---|---|---|
| Sept 11 | Hotel Kossak | Plac Kossaka 1 Old Town 30-106 +48 12 379 59 00 reservation # | |
| | Vodka Tasting | Szpitalna 1 +48 5021 50526 reservation # | 1800 |
| 12 | Pierogi Cooking Olga | Plac Jana Matejki 13 +48 693 699 683 confirm # | 1100 |
| | Cruise Vistula River Aqua Fun | Bulwar Czerwieńskí 172 | 1800 |
| 13 | Wielicka Salt Mine | hotel pickup | 0930 |
| | Thermal Baths | hotel pickup | 1600 |
| 14 | Da Vinci Lady with an Ermine | National Museum | |
| 15 | Zackopane, Slovakia Tree top walk | Hotel Pickup | 1000 |
| 16 | Free/Recovery Day | search for fire eating dragon | |
| 17 | LH #1385 | KRK - FRA | 1245 - 1425 |
| | LH #1040 | FRA - CDG | 1615 - 1730 |
| | Car Service to hotel | Confirm # | |
| 17 | Les Patios du Marais 1 | +33 1 70 37 14 26 reservation # | |
| 18 | French Croissant Baking | Maison Fleuret 7 Rue de Bearn +33 143229198 Le Cafe Chinos on corner printout | 1300 |
| 19 | Giverney | bus @ Pl du Trocadero | 0915 |
| 20 | Picasso, Pierre Lachaise | | |
| | Don Pasquale Opera | Garnier printout | 1930 |
| 21 | Stroll about Explore | | |
| | Don Giovanni Opera | Opera Bastille printout | 1930 |
| 22 | Wander about the Marais | | |
| 23 | DL 3221 | CDG - SLC | 1010 - 1245 |
| | DL #2246 | SLC - SAN | 1520 - 1610 |
| | ride share home | | |

Confirmation and E ticket
**DELTA**
GGVYFD
0067967380860
**LOT**
2BRIST
0807884060007
**LUFTHANSA**
2BUESS
2207883401915
**VIATOR Customer Care** (travel source for booking tours and events)
702 939 9839
**GYG customer service** (travel source for booking tours and events) +1 844 326 5840

SAMPLE ITINERARY

**Embassies**

Prague
 Tržistĕ 15
 118 01 Praha - Malá
 Czech Republic
 Switchboard: (+420) 257 022 000

Poland
 Aleje Ujazdowskie 29/31
 00-540 Warsaw Poland
 Tel: +48 22 504 2000

Paris
 2 avenue Gabriel
 75008 Paris, France
 (33) (1) 431 12 2222

MASA (Flight evacuation insurance)
 800 643 9023
 Member #xxxx

175

# ACKNOWLEDGMENTS

Writing may be a solitary act, but bringing a book into the world is anything but. I owe heartfelt thanks to the many humans (and a few persistent cats who improved my one-handed typing skills) who helped this book find its way to completion.

My deepest gratitude goes to Jerry Strayve, a steadfast supporter who believed in this project from the very beginning. I am also deeply thankful to the wise and generous members of the San Diego Writing Group—especially Tamara Merrill and Craig McCleod—for their thoughtful feedback and encouragement. Deep appreciation to Cornelia Feye, who took the manuscript over the last hurdle.

A special thank you to the talented Tom Lien, who designed the beautiful cover that makes this book far more attractive than anything I could have imagined, and to Trisha Gooch, for her sharp editorial eye.

Thanks to Stefanie Blue, who somehow managed to wrangle me into sitting still long enough for a portrait.

Warm thanks go to the many friends who offered encouragement along the way

To my brother Joe and his wife, Vonne, thank you for insisting I address accessibility and making sure the work was more inclusive and complete. Sean and Laura, your love is a constant.

Finally, to my feline co-authors, who selflessly offered their "assistance" by sprawling across the keyboard, claiming lap space at critical moments, and ensuring I became proficient at typing with one hand—this book bears your paw prints in more ways than one

To all of you: this book carries a piece of your spirit, humor, and heart. Thank you.

# ABOUT THE AUTHOR

Dr. Mary Strobbe began life riding horses barefoot and bareback. Earning a degree in nursing, she began adventures as an Army Nurse during the Vietnam era. Returning to college, she graduated with a PhD in Psychology, enabling her to teach at a Community College. Critical thinking and acceptance of diversity were the core principles of her courses. During those early years of travel, she drove solo throughout the U.S.A. Following widowhood, she continues her solo adventures and has been to over 60 countries. Through tales of her escapades, she encourages others to explore the world, seeking out other cultures, way of life, and the local cuisine. At 80, she continues to explore the world. She lives in San Diego with judgmental feline companions. Dr. Strobbe can be reached at Travelingsolo.withMary@gmail.com

www.ingramcontent.com/pod-product-compliance
Lightning Source LLC
LaVergne TN
LVHW041937070526
838199LV00051BA/2829